Ten Thousand Whispers

A Guide to Conscious Creation

Ten Thousand Whispers

A Guide to Conscious Creation

Lynda Madden Dahl

The Woodbridge Group

Ten Thousand Whispers

First printing, August 1995
Second printing, April 1997

Library of Congress Cataloging-in-Publication Data
Dahl, Lynda Madden, 1943—
   Ten thousand whispers: a guide to conscious creation / by Lynda Madden Dahl
      p.   cm.
   Originally published: Eugene, OR : Windsong Pub., 1995.
   Includes bibliographical references.
   ISBN 1-889964-06-9
   1. Mental suggestion—Miscellanea. 2. Success—Psychic aspects.
   3. New Thought. I. Title.
[BF1156.S8D34 1997]
131—dc21   97-1153
                                                                           CIP

The Woodbridge Group
PO Box 849 ✦ Eugene OR ✦ 97440 ✦ USA
(541) 683-6731 ✦ fax (541) 683-1084

Dedication

This book is dedicated to the pioneers of consciousness, the people who, by simply changing their minds about the structure of our reality, will bring unprecedented change into the world.

L.M.D.

Contents

*Before It Enters Physical Reality...Altering the Body
...Mind-Communicating With Your Inner Self...A
Psy-Time Exercise: Meeting Your Inner Self...Flexing
Our Inner Senses*

In Acknowledgment

When one person offers unqualified support in countless ways and through whatever means, words become but vague translations of deeply felt gratitude. Without my love Stan at my side, I could not, at this time, hold title of author—it's that simple. And without his appreciation for and understanding of the Seth material, I would not have a fine edge against which to hone my ideas and conclusions.

In many ways, I owe my Seth-reader friends and acquaintances the world over similar gratitude. We're learning together and comparing insights, and their breakthroughs in thought fuel mine into new or more complete understandings.

Our shared philosophical basis is the gift of Seth, Jane Roberts and Robert F. Butts—and what a wondrous gift it is, replete with knowledge and excitement and hope. To this triad I offer a silent salute in friendship and gratitude.

L.M.D.

You seek the Holy Grail of consciousness when there are really ten thousand whispers of reality.

—The Committee

As in <u>your</u> terms the cavemen ventured out into the daylight of the earth, so there is a time for man to venture out into a greater knowledge of his subjective reality, to explore the dimensions of selfhood and go beyond the small areas of himself in which he has thus far found shelter.

—*Seth*, The "Unknown" Reality, Volume One, *Session 684*

Introduction

The radio talk show host inhaled quickly and let the next zinger fly. "How can you possibly believe, Lynda, that a ring you *say* you lost could 'rematerialize' (big quote marks drawn by impatient fingers slashed the air) thirty miles from the scene of the loss?" *Uh, guess I hallucinated the experience, Jer.* "Well, Jerry, as we come to understand the concept of simultaneous time and the creative abilities of consciousness..."

"And how can you believe you created a million dollars through what you call conscious creation?" *I dunno. Guess you had to be there.* "Well, Jerry, as we come to understand the concept of simultaneous time and the creative abilities of consciousness..."

"Hold on a minute, honey. You honestly canceled your health insurance because you <u>know</u> you'll never need it? Now isn't that stretching things a bit?" *Well, sweetie, it depends on your perspective.*

"No, Jerry, not at all. It gets down to consciousness and time and..."

I watched in awe as Jerry turned into the avenger of the common, the voice of the conventional, the arbiter of the unthinking. With cape flying he soared across the heavens, aglow with the flush of victory. He had slain the interloper and secured the mediocre for yet another generation. He felt damn good.

But the universe works in mysterious ways, at least in dreams. Jerry had flown too close to the heat of new thought, and it was his demise. His cape disintegrated and his stubby body melted. He limped and dripped through the sky, a mere stunted mortal in the end.

I awoke chuckling. I felt damn good.

Since the publication of my first book, *Beyond the Winning Streak: Using Conscious Creation to Consistently Win at Life*, I've been on numerous radio and television shows, and I only met Jerry in my dreams. Most hosts are gracious and curious, if not completely accepting of the idea that we literally create our lives based on our thoughts, attitudes and beliefs. Their audiences are the same. I noticed that if I have time to explain the basic structure of our reality in concrete terms, they click in, turn on, light up more quickly; but if I ride the surface too long, their natural cynicism overcomes good manners. And why not? I understand their position— I've been there myself. As a former twenty-year computer industry veteran, I am well acquainted with their attitude. It was mine for years.

There is a phrase from the song "I Am Woman" that goes, "...and I know too much to go back and pretend." As I explained in *Beyond the Winning Streak*, I did materialize a ring lost many miles from where it reappeared, I did create a million dollars after choosing wealth as my road to freedom, and I did cancel my health insurance because I know I'll never need it. And I've accomplished dozens of other things through conscious creation, also. It doesn't take a two-by-four to get my attention: Something of significance is going on here. So why would I choose to go back and pretend otherwise?

I'd have to forget that there is a structure to this reality that can be used to our advantage, helping us to bring abundance in all things into our lives. I'd have to try not to remember that we can use this structure to fulfill our desires and wishes, because that's why it's in place. And I'd have to deny its logic—not logic honed by our present limited ideas of what is and is not possible, but one that is far greater in scope, much grander in design, larger than life as we know it. This logic was initiated at the birth of the universe, an integral part of the vastness called All That Is, or God. However, it's a logic that escapes notice because it's obvious only when we become aware of it.

By going back and pretending, I'd have to play victim once more to life's whims and join the billions of people who have died believing in the powerlessness of the individual. Through the centuries they've paraded, participating in the dramas of wars, ghettos, famines, crime and commonly accepted illnesses. They've scurried through the after-dark streets of New York, London, Bogota and Our Town, metaphorically genuflecting to their favorite icon of safety as their fear rose with the moon. In self-defense they've built bigger weapons, developed more medicines and prayed to the current god of protection. And in spite of their safeguards, the majority of those who have inhabited the face of the earth have died from disease or slaughter.

So goes our world through the millennia, and so it will continue until we change our ideas of what does and does not constitute reality, and until we understand our participation in events. If we continue to choose not to believe we have the slightest impact on the creation of our lives, we can't possibly break the cycle. We will follow in the footsteps of our forefathers, looking to an outside source to bail us out of our latest trouble, but, instead, causing repeated tragedy. And how many more can we sustain, globally and individually?

A Blue, Blue Easter

Along with dozens of other moviegoers on Easter day in 1994, I cried out at the horror of the Holocaust as portrayed in Steven Spielberg's film, *Schindler's List*. My unfinished popcorn sat forgotten in my lap as I wiped at tears staining my cheeks. I sat mesmerized by scene after scene of indignity, indecency, terror and death. My heart ached with sadness at the gross violations of human against human—acts perpetrated in the name of superiority. My nerves froze with the hopelessness, the helplessness emanating from the wide screen.

But even with great emotion roiling through my mind, I suspected my tears were of a different weather than those of my companions in that high-tech auditorium. I suspected they still believed in evil, in victimization, in a god outside themselves. I suspected most of the Easter day moviegoers still believed in random acts of violence, in vulnerability, in unfortunate circumstances and bad luck. But of course they did, if they agreed with most of the world. And that's what caused my tears.

Over the past ten years I've become intimately familiar with the most freeing, exciting news ever; news that's been around since the beginning of time, but buried under the debris of civilization-imposed ignorance for long, long centuries. It casts individuals and their participation in events in a very different light, one that suggests power, purpose and meaning. And in that movie theater I shed tears for the human race, wondering just how much longer it was going to take us to break the bonds of limiting past beliefs and move into our heritage—the right to consciously develop life on earth in whatever ways we see fit and proper by understanding and using our inherent capabilities.

So, where did we go wrong? In the only place we can ever get off track: our belief systems. We have chosen to believe that we're problem children from the outset, in conflict with a parent god; life happens by chance in a mechanistic universe; a dark force is at play in our world; and only God can secure our peace and only science can heal our hurting bodies.

On the surface of physical reality these assumptions stand tall, cloaked in apparent validity. We study the world at large and find evil incarnate—why else would unspeakable horrors continue? We look at an individual's inability to make the pain disappear—surely such transformations are only in the power of the Godhead or science? We gasp at human acts of nastiness toward all living things—isn't man degenerate by nature, angels gone awry? Given these assumptions and our belief in them, the road to global happiness seems remote indeed, fairy-tale illusion of the highest order.

But there is another way to view the world and our participation in it that maps a road toward peace and value fulfillment that is indeed attainable. This view affords we the people the status of whole, complete beings now and evermore, here on earth for quite a different learning objective than present-day theologies and sciences suggest. It drops the power of creation into the lap of each individual who has ever been or ever will be born into physical life, and it suggests that, once we learn what we're dealing with, we'll finally understand the genesis of events. And through this understanding, we will bring great change into our world.

The Gift of the Gods

I left mainstream America in thought, if not in deed, about eleven years ago. Firmly ensconced in the computer industry for almost fifteen years at that point and riding a wave of executive success, I hardly seemed a candidate for a stunning alteration in belief systems. But, there I was, along with my partner and love, Stan, and thousands of others, questioning the very foundation of world assumptions. My own personal upheaval of beliefs started when I read a book called *Seth Speaks* by the brilliant author Jane Roberts. The next book by Jane and Seth that I read, *The Nature of Personal Reality*, clinched it. I would never see our world or our reality through the blinders of the past again.

But who or what is Seth, anyway? According to his own definition, he's an energy essence personality no longer focused in physical reality. You might think of him as an intelligence residing outside time and space. He made himself known to acclaimed writer Jane Roberts and her artist/writer husband Robert Butts in 1963 while they were experimenting with a Ouija board for a book project of Jane's. Neither had had previous interest in or experience with the metaphysical and were quite unprepared for Seth's breakthrough introduction of himself.

But, given time and the quality of what they were getting on the board, Rob and Jane loosened their concerns, and Jane then allowed Seth to speak through her voice instead of the cumbersome Ouija board. With Rob transcribing Seth's words, they established a three-way working relationship that led to almost 1,800 sessions held over twenty-plus years, until Jane's death in 1984. Some of the sessions were specifically dictated by Seth as book material and now comprise nine published books and one yet-to-be-printed manuscript. Other sessions were incorporated, whole, in piece or in theory, into fourteen published books and one unpublished manuscript written by Jane, works not orchestrated by Seth.[1] Then there are more than sixteen other manuscripts waiting to be compiled from Seth's discussions recorded during ESP classes Jane held for many years, and from sessions originally deleted from transcribed material.

The Seth material challenges the very fabric of accepted global thought from which most theories and conclusions are presently drawn, especially the "law" of cause and effect. According to Seth, we are given the gift of the gods—the gift of creativity. He says there is only one rule of physical existence, and that is the fact that we literally create our individual realities through our thoughts, attitudes and beliefs. Events don't happen *to* us; we *cause* them by what we expect to see in our world and our lives. Every event we encounter and participate in is a physical reflection of what we think and feel. The implications of this statement are startling, for if we have created the reality of our individual and global lives, then surely we can change what we don't like.

Seth didn't present the world with the Great Cosmic Bible; he whispered universal truths into our ears. If a person is looking for the Ten Commandments of metaphysics, he or she will not find them here. The material's non-dogmatic, non-superficial stance, coupled with information that astounds the intellect at times, has captured many readers' attention—approximately seven million of them, in fact. Prestigious Yale University selected Jane's and Rob's work for their archives, a tribute to its quality and importance. Interestingly, it's the only metaphysical body of work housed in the archives and one of the most visited, according to a Yale spokesperson.

But the bottom line is, does it work? Can we really change our lives by changing our thoughts? Do we literally have the power of creation at our fingertips? Run those questions by any number of Seth readers and be prepared for some evocative answers. In my case, as I wrote in my first book, by using conscious creation I moved myself out of a marketing manager's job with Apple Computer, Inc. into a vice presidency with another computer industry firm, and then went on to make a lot of money—all because of what Seth says is possible if we but know how to do it.

Ten Thousand Whispers is not about the Seth material per se, although some basic concepts will be covered. It's about each of us, you and me. It's about our heritage, our abilities, our future. It's about our power, our rights, our value fulfillment. It's about having what we want, becoming whom we choose. And it's about our civilization and how we can contribute to its great purpose and intent through new understandings.

Summer of My Discontent

The summer of my twelfth year found me in an upper Michigan Bible camp. For the previous five or so years, my mother, two of my sisters and I had been attending a fundamentalist Christian church, although in the 1950s neither the adjective nor the meaning behind it were known to the general public. No different than most religious institutions, much of what was taught had to be taken on faith and interpretation, the latter being the purview of whatever slice of Christianity held your former.

I remember running to the first-aid station which my mother, a registered nurse, managed, and pulling her aside for a quiet conference. Several of my new friends had been spouting religious doctrine that had been taught to us in class that morning as though it was unquestioned gospel (pun intended). I was quite upset by their casual acceptance of the information and thought my mom could help explain away shadows of doubt lingering around my mind's periphery.

She tried, but I wasn't buying it as easily as she'd hoped. Finally, in exasperation tinged with humor, she said, "Honey, you're never going to be religious. You question too much!" Nine years later with the death of my mother, I decided the same thing. She had died after years of backbreaking work and little happiness to show for it, and my relentless questions about how that could happen to such a noble soul fissured into a break with the church.

If three words can possibly describe the inner need of an individual, mine would be, "I must understand." I can't help it, I was born that way. My mind insists on understanding, not simply accepting. In recent years I've learned to mesh the intellect and intuitive, paying both their due, but when I first started reading the Seth material, my skittish movement toward or away from it was up for grabs. Fortunately, Seth made sense on a hard-core physical level as well as with the softer, less provable esoterica; so I stuck around.

As I am of logic-oriented persuasion, the information that convinced me that if conscious creation can work at all, it is because of these, are Seth's concepts of consciousness, simultaneous time and probabilities. No longer was I told simply to have faith that all would work out; I was told *why*, if I had faith, it would all work out. That information answers so many questions about the universal structure that allows and supports the creation of everything—events, material items, bodies, our world, the environment, indeed, all of physical reality—that it made it easier for me to give conscious creation a try.

I love the term "haphazard constructions." Seth used it a couple of times in his books, and it captured my imagination. Paraphrased, he says much of what we see in the world is a result of beliefs gone haywire. Because we don't know we're creating it all, we don't do it with finesse. We blunder into the creation of events and then must face their results, and it ain't pretty at times. Illness, accidents, poverty, victimization, aggression, loveless relationships...the list goes on. Haphazard constructions made manifest.

So, maybe it's time we drop currently accepted conventional thinking from the A list, since it hasn't exactly transformed our world into one of brotherly love and abundance for all, and move on to unconventional ideas that just may do the trick.

In *Beyond the Winning Streak* I told of my search for answers, the ongoing doubts that assailed me at every turn, and the culmination of my conscious creation efforts after several years of trying. After I completed the book, I realized it was my version of chapter one of conscious creation. My need to understand continues and, by its very nature, leads me into new challenges and further insights. This book is meant to be my version of chapter two of conscious creation. Many others around the globe are writing their own chapters, if not on paper, certainly in their psyches, as they also grapple with the intricacies of consciously living in a reality constructed of thought.

1

The responsibility for your life and your world is indeed yours. It has not been forced upon you by some outside agency. You form your own dreams, and you form your own physical reality. The world is what you are. It is the physical materialization of the inner selves which have formed it.
—Seth, The Seth Material, *Chapter 18*

The 180-Degree Turn

Conscious creation is nothing more than learning to live in physical reality under the guidelines established for it. It's a fancy name for living naturally within the universal structure that supports all creation, conscious or otherwise. The whole purpose of conscious creation is to break the bonds of past limiting beliefs about what is and is not possible in our lives and reach for the stars with new knowledge under our belts. It is, in essence, becoming adept at manipulating within our reality to manifest goals of choice.

Defining conscious creation isn't that difficult; understanding its subtleties is more complex. To consciously create what we want out of life takes a complete reorientation of thinking, a 180-degree evolution away from what we've been taught is real, lo these many years. We're so used to believing that events happen outside ourselves, formed by luck, fate and other people, that we never question the validity of the belief. It becomes an assumption, and a very powerful, limiting one. The most exhilarating gift we can give ourselves is the knowledge that we are lowercase gods, with complete creative control over our lives. From this point of understanding, we can then build a platform of thought which allows us to radically change our circumstances.

When we decide to take credit for the events we experience, we bump against the patterned thinking of the masses. Their beliefs in individual powerlessness hit us every time we read a newspaper, watch television, listen to conversations. If you want to reinforce the idea you're a victim of circumstances, no problem. The vehicles are endless and constant in today's society, including what's found in much metaphysical material. So, most of what we'll be doing for the rest of this book is to help break the hypnotic focus on what we've been conditioned to accept, and come into our own through a reorientation of thinking.

Learning to Tell Truth From Snake Oil

After reading *Beyond the Winning Streak,* a man called to tell me he was so excited by the possibilities of conscious creation that he had decided to double the size of his office in preparation for the inflow of business he was sure would occur. I grew uneasy listening to him as it became apparent that he'd only given the structure behind conscious creation a cursory nod of the head.

I felt he was flying by the seat of the superficial, running with the hope that all would work out to match his desire just because he'd read it in a book. In other words, he'd not changed his thoughts in any significant way that would allow success; he'd simply chosen one idea of the many that comprise the concept of conscious creation and called it his savior. Four months later he closed down his additional space due to lack of business, somewhat sick at heart and definitely doubting the validity of consciously creating his reality.

Another person told me of losing his home to bankruptcy and

believing the universe had set the stage for such a wallop in order to tell him it was time to release his attachment to it. A woman friend suggested that a car accident in which she was injured was put into place by the universe so that she would learn to slow down and take life easier. I heard another woman tell a group of friends that she never wears the color red because of the negative effect it has on other people's auras. According to a booth exhibitor I met at a metaphysical trade show, the reason some people were challenging the veracity of the products he was selling was because of "karma." Another exhibitor at the same show was promoting the idea that he could teach people to tap into the unified field, and then all their beliefs would automatically change because they would become one with the field.

The "New Age" is adrift in misunderstandings. Sure, new ideas have blown the ceiling off mainstream thought. Yes, pioneering concepts have seeded ground long fallow. But, like the first frontier towns of the Old West, there's no understanding of basic organization, no obvious order, no apparent way to tell truth from snake oil. Never mind that we're having one heck of a good time exploring all the boisterous possibilities. That's not the issue. The issue is, are we changing? Do our personal lives reflect the material items and feelings we wish to experience? Does our global life reflect the calmness and attunement we've been told is possible? Have we learned the true nature of this physical reality, and are we becoming skilled at working within it to make events of choice happen?

If not, the villain isn't necessarily whimsy. Maybe it's lack of understanding. The kernels of truth have been popped with common corn and tumbled into the bowl of new thought. But, to our inexperienced eye, they all look alike. So we test one here, one there, intrigued with the flavor, but nonetheless still stuck—in the old job, the lack of money, the failing body, the loveless relationship.

The new spirituality of the last several years offers an anchor in our sometimes turbulent lives, a checkpoint for what we call our spiritual growth. We feel we're finally getting the hang of living in this reality, finding our purpose and life's meaning. But too often our developing views windsurf the edges of knowledge about our reality when what we need to do is dip to its depths in order to understand what *causes* creation, and our role in the process—because what we create becomes our private lives, our societies and our civilization.

Bumper-Sticker Stuck

"You create your own reality," Seth said for the first time in 1964. That phrase, destined to launch what's come to be called the New Age, went on to become one of the most popular one-liners of the next three decades, repeated zillions of times by millions of people. But understood? That's another issue.

It reminds me of a conversation I had recently that went something like this: "But, Lynda, you *can't* tell people they create their realities. I mean, after all, *look* at their lives, for heaven's sake! Even if they believe it, what happens? They feel guilt or blame for what they've created. No, it will never work." And this from a man who has been around metaphysics for over twenty years and made quite a name for himself in the process.

But it does point up a major issue. If this guy doesn't recognize the liberating, life-changing power behind the words, "You create your own reality," why not? He's been exposed to hundreds of acclaimed forward thinkers, he's mingled with them professionally and personally, he's written books about them. The problem seems to be, at least from my perspective after having read many of the ideas espoused by these people, that they still believe in one reality and one self that is unfolded through linear time, with the main purpose of life being to grow spiritually. And those beliefs automatically place boundaries on the range and breadth of their thinking. They may talk a bigger picture, but their new ideas are colored by what their senses and historical thought systems suggest is real.

Generally speaking, what many metaphysical people believe is: 1) We create our own reality—sometimes; 2) there is an orderly past, present and future, with one moment and one year flowing into the next; 3) we are explicitly in physical existence to become more spiritual; 4) sure, the universe is here to support, and it's also here to teach us lessons, whether we like them or not; 5) we can be impacted by the energy and thoughts of others.

According to Seth: 1) We create our own reality, without exception; 2) time is simultaneous, with the past, present and future active, accessible and changeable in this very moment; 3) we already are spiritual beings, here in physical reality for deeper reasons and purposes; 4) the universe is here to support, and the lessons we face are placed in time by each of *us* for our individual reasons; 5) we have complete creative control over what we experience, and that means we cannot be impacted by another, in any way, unless we allow it.

The difference in these two sets of assumptions spells the difference between whether or not we reach individual freedom and world peace. The first set carries us beyond mainstream thinking, but not far enough to make a sustained impact. Although draped in new thought, it still too closely parallels the myth of a personified exterior controller and a hapless individual adrift in a universe run by luck and happenstance to support dramatic change.

When we force completely new views of reality into that old mold, we lose the power of the message. As long as we believe we're at the mercy of fate, the universe, linear time or other people *for any reason*, we will never shed our beliefs in vulnerability and victimization, and so will continue to experience them. It can be no other way in a reality where what we believe is made manifest.

So, let's start our search for answers and change by first studying the construct of the universe in general and physical reality in particular, or better said—since tomes could be written about both subjects—let's select those bits of information for discussion that help us craft a new set of lenses through which to view life and, by default, teach us about conscious creation.

All That Is

"The Beginning," to use an accepted if distorted term, was a condition where All That Is was not fulfilled. It existed in a state of conscious being as a psychic pyramid gestalt,[1] but without the means to express itself. It was loaded with probabilities and possibilities desiring actualization, but ways to produce them were not apparent. All That Is saw an infinity of probable, conscious individuals, and understood all possible developments around each; and It was consumed with the desire to create both the individuals and their infinite probabilities. This overwhelming need to create, and the expectation that a way would be found, culminated in a magnificent flash of creation as psychic energy from All That Is burst forth into actualization. In so doing, All That Is gave birth to individualized consciousness.

The connection between each of us as individualized consciousness and our creator can never be severed. As a literal part of All That Is, as a portion of All That Is that knows Itself as us, we retain memory of It's great creativity and desire, and they become ours. We draw upon It's overall energy constantly, since our existence depends on it; and as our source, It is there when we need help. Even the most minute particle of All That Is carries the innate knowledge of the whole. So, while we are very much individual, our individuality can better be described as a distinct portion of All That Is made to look separate.

From All That Is springs all worlds, all realities, all selves. It is a living, loving, expanding energy gestalt of consciousness that *thinks* itself into shapes, events and things. Everything within our universe—space, time, matter and forces—emerges and is molded from this energy of consciousness. Everything we see in our reality is consciousness allowing itself to be made physical for its own expression. So, it goes without saying that "dead matter" is a non sequitur. It also goes without saying that consciousness cannot die. It can, and does, change states, but it can't be annihilated.

Desire and expectation are the basis for any of All That Is's created structures; hence, they are the overriding impetuses that direct and shape our lives, since we share characteristics with It by nature of our heritage. Desire and expectation lead us to create further structures which reflect the wholeness of All That Is...and the cycle of creativity and the expansion of All That Is continues, partially through us.

Consciousness Units

All That Is is consciousness. Consciousness is all that is. The implications of those two statements would change the face of civilization if understood and accepted. What they suggest is that everything we see and experience is built of consciousness, and everything we see and experience is a part of All That Is. All realities, worlds, events, matter and creatures are extensions of All That Is, literally formed from It and by It. Nothing appears anywhere in the universe without the building blocks of consciousness behind its creation and within its structure.

But how? Does God wave a cosmic wand and voilà!, another event, another material object is created? Or is there, dare we say, *logic* associated with manifestation? According to Seth, that is the case. That we don't understand it is our problem; the mechanics, if you will, have always been in place, and we've used them whether we knew it or not.

It seems that consciousness is composed of "mental" units of consciousness (CUs), the smallest possible unit of All That Is. Held within each CU is the knowledge of the universe and the "history" and pattern of All That Is. Since these units are parts of It, they are nonphysical energy that is aware of itself. Each CU has the built-in ability to organize, expand and develop along any lines it chooses. It is charged with a propensity toward expression and a great desire to fulfill itself through creativity. According to Seth, CUs never become physical particles themselves, but all physical matter emerges from them. They build the atoms and molecules found in our world, along with everything else.

Now, an interesting thing about these CUs: They are found in all places at once and exist outside time and space. And because they are not formed under the rules of time and space, or three-dimensional reality, and are everywhere concurrently, they are free to be clairvoyant and precognitive. Not only that, but their awareness of all organizations of which they are a part allows them to pass great amounts of information back and forth between individuals and groups, eschewing time and space boundaries.

These All-That-Is's in miniature are endowed with unpredictability, which is extremely important because anything less would ultimately result in stagnation. This unpredictability, by its very nature, supports infinite probabilities and patterns. Consciousness, in order to create and develop, has to have the ultimate freedom to be what it chooses, when it chooses.

CUs form themselves into groupings and systems that they themselves initiate, becoming their own camouflage, or disguise. From these groupings and systems come everything from realities to rocks, offering the participating CUs a platform for experience—the whole point of their being. And our being is a direct result of their being. Seth says CUs form what we think of as the mind, and then they form the brain and body (the mind is resident throughout the body and beyond, not just in the brain, he says).

But CUs don't just form us, they *permeate* us while still residing outside of time and space. And that's why, because of a CU's propensity to know everything of which it is a part, every cell in our body knows instantly what is happening with its counterparts and every mind is in constant touch with all others. It's the communication system of the CUs that makes our reality run smoothly.

Greater Selves

The universe is nothing if not organized. While All That Is is assuredly all that is, It chooses to diversify into functional groupings with various purposes and intents. The one we need most to understand is the construct of our individual greater selves. (All That Is is pure energy, and this energy cannot be divided like a sliced apple. In fact, it can't be divided at all. But, onward we go, trying like crazy to make sense of something far beyond our complete knowing.)

First comes the definition of "self." We automatically assign such a designation to physical beings alive in physical reality. But that is a very limiting definition, at least in universal terms. A self is any energy gestalt bounded by a definite border. That's what humans are, although our borders are not delineated by the physical body, as one might think. They are psychic in nature and extend far beyond the body. Indeed, it's our *mind* that is our true bordered self. Our bodies can disappear and we will still be our self.

Mind doesn't need a physical body to "be." Mind creates the body as a physical symbol of itself, but it's only one symbol of many used by the mind to convey its diversity. In fact, there are selves alive and well throughout the universe who have never directly participated in physical reality, and yet, through desire and expectation, create their lives in the molds of their choice, just as we who participate in physicality do.

Our greater selves are of that category. They are energy gestalts of tremendous power. Each one of them, through the same creative process as All That Is—indeed, as a part of All That Is—creates many other selves, both physical and nonphysical, and gives them life through their astounding energy. A greater self can have numerous physical selves alive throughout what we perceive as historical linear time, all under its wing of protection and assistance whether or not those physical selves realize it.

The Inner Self

Keeping in mind that there really are no divisions between All That Is and its creations, we will continue to insist upon dividing the whole of It into something somewhat understandable to our current methods of comprehension.

While each of us is fueled by a greater self, of which we are but one of its many creations, the conduit for that energy is our inner self. An inner self is a portion of a greater self's consciousness assigned the specific task of creating a physical self and then keeping that self clearly pinpointed in its pre-chosen space/time continuum.

Our inner self is very intimate. It keeps the definition of our body intact, its energy sustains us, its advice guides us, and its creative abilities build our physical environment based on what we tell it to do through our thoughts and beliefs. Indeed, our inner self is so much a part of us that it extends itself into physical reality as and through our conscious mind and *becomes* our environment.

When we ask for assistance or call for help, it's our inner self who directly responds. It's the one who extends the helping hand, leads us into "coincidences" that answer our needs, suggests we not give up so soon. It uses many vehicles for communication, such as dreams, intuition, inspiration, insight, inner voice and impulses. Without an inner self we could not function in physical reality, since it not only guides us, it keeps us alive through an inflow of its energy. All of our bodily and psychic unconscious activity is directed by our inner self, from the balance of body chemistry to the creation of our dreams. We are a literal part of it, formed in the inner world, yet appearing in the outer world.

As magnificent as our physical reality is, only this "small" portion of the overall universal consciousness, or All That Is, need take part in its creation. The creative energy that forms our world comes from our collective inner selves, those expanded portions of each of us residing outside of time and space. We, in turn, and all living things of this earth are imbued with our *own* creative energy—and inherent within that energy is the constant desire and need to express ourselves through continual manifestation.

Electromagnetic Energy Units

Consciousness, whether it's composed of one unit of consciousness or, like humans, many, emanates electromagnetic energy (EE) units with every subjective experience. That is, with every thought, emotion or mental picture, consciousness emits EE units. These units, imbued with consciousness themselves, have a unique electromagnetic reality which can combine with others of like intensity. They become the basic carriers of perception, found just beneath the range of physical matter, yet giving birth to it and becoming a part of it. They are the entryway into physical matter.

EE units are built up in response to emotional intensity. The stronger the thought or feeling, the greater the size, stability and strength of their magnetic nature. They will attract others of the same nature, forming a larger and larger magnetic field. The stronger the intensity of the field, the faster and more stable the physical materialization of the structure that has been designed for actualization by consciousness.

And what consciousness initiates, organizes and projects the EE units into physical reality? Our inner selves. What motivates them to do what they do with specific EE units? Our emotions and thoughts. Our inner selves create form based on the concentrated energy generated by us through a thought, belief or feeling.

Idea Construction

Our world and everything in it is idea construction, or the transformation of ideas into physical reality. The universe is made up of the raw material of energy, or consciousness, as we discussed. But it must be converted into usable form in order to enter this reality as matter or event. Ideas are the mental catalysts that transform that energy into a substance that conforms to the physical world's needs and specifications.

Ideas, or thoughts, hold great power, because if held long enough in the conscious mind, they create structure in this world. Everything we see surrounding us is an idea—or an idea construction—that has been thought into existence, and that includes all material items and events we encounter. In fact, our body is our greater self's idea construction of how it sees us translated into flesh. *We* are ideas made physical through the molding of energy. All matter formations are, in effect, psychological objects since they are formed in the mind first. Matter does not give rise to consciousness; consciousness births matter.

The simple amoebae, being consciousness just like all other organisms, create idea constructions from energy, also. According to Jane Roberts, the precise ideas they receive are constructed almost simultaneously because they receive so few and all are needed to ensure survival.[2] Man, on the other hand, finds it impossible to construct all of his ideas physically because of the great numbers of complex thoughts he deals with, and so developed an ego that would make the necessary choices.

The environment that each of us experiences is the overall idea construction of what we choose to translate into matter. We only perceive our own constructions (remember, we create our individual realities), but because we agree on some basic ideas, the appearance of the environment has coherence. Our private constructions seem to overlap ones created by others and we agree on certain shared parameters, but make no mistake about it: My reality is my reality, and yours is yours. Each resides in its individual, personal psychic space or space continuum, and so is very much unique and apart—yet with the suggestion of being one.

Seth says, "Physical objects cannot exist unless they exist in a definite perspective and space continuum. But each individual creates his own space continuum...Each individual actually creates an entirely different object."[3] For instance, five people will view what they believe to be the same table, but, actually, five tables are projected into time and space, of the same general format but with individual touches. When we walk into a room, we telepathically agree on the placement and dimensions of the table and all other objects and people in that room, and then we individually, in our own space continuums, build the scene to match our understandings. The result: a scene that is camouflaged to look like one place in one time and one space.

Camouflage, in fact, is all we ever see. The elements that create our world are camouflages of the basic elements of the universe that reside in the inner world beyond time and space. The whole of physical reality is composed of camouflage patterns reflective of patterns of thought residing "somewhere else"; that is, each piece of camouflage has a counterpart in inner reality.

Inner Senses

Always in our logic-oriented universe there is a framework behind any action that supports its occurrence, from communication with our inner selves to the literal creation of physical reality. Nothing happens without there being a structure in place that supports the activity. That structure is based in the inner senses. The inner senses are the means by which our physical reality is built and maintained and the conduit for information between the outer world and the inner world. They are the tools used by the universe to make things happen. All the knowledge found in the physical world enters it through the inner senses.

There are nine inner senses listed by Seth in chapter nineteen of *The Seth Material,* but he assures us they do not stand alone and shouldn't really be viewed as individual. He says we use all of them constantly as a whole, and without the whole it would be impossible for anything to be actualized, anywhere.

Since time and space don't exist for the inner senses, they have no problem communicating across those illusory boundaries, and this is where their tremendous value lies. Because they transcend space/time, they are free to deal in concepts and results not limited by the coloration of narrowed thinking.

Not that distortions don't occur, but it's not the inner material that's flawed. The information received through the inner senses is clear in that it reflects reality as it exists independently of what the physical senses perceive. However, as information is filtered through a person's belief system, it is colored accordingly. For instance, are there really angels? Sure, to the people who see them. Do all people see angels? No, only if they believe in the possibility of angels, want to experience a dramatic occurrence, or select the event for some other reason, consciously or otherwise.

In fact, one person might interpret the same construct as a nature spirit, or ghost, or vision, or extraterrestrial, or whatever he or she will allow to manifest. The information that formed the "angel" is valid, however, no matter what its packaging. It came through the inner senses, and while the manifestation is up for definition, depending on who is doing the viewing, its emergence into physical reality is a valid event.

When we consciously use the inner senses, we transcend physical reality and play in the universe unfettered by restrictive beliefs. We can enter other realities, clearly communicate with our inner selves, develop telepathic, precognitive and clairvoyant abilities and sense the workings of the universe. We become aware of our multidimensionality, aware that physical reality is a very small portion of our existence, and aware that we have at our disposal an incredible tool to use in everyday life to consciously manipulate physical reality to our liking.

By flexing the muscles of the inner senses, we allow the flow of intuition, impulses, inspiration and insights from our inner self to become more obvious, more pronounced and more frequent. Using our minds, the meeting place of the inner and outer worlds, we can float beneath the camouflage of our reality, camouflage created by the inner senses, and catch a glimpse of what lies beyond the illusion.

Simultaneous Time

It seems that linear time is but a tool that we, as consciousness in a physical reality, have chosen in order to experience the results of our idea constructions. The point of linear time is to be able to see and feel our creations in slow motion, so to speak, and then decide what works and what doesn't in our lives. That is its primary value. Time has no purpose other than to bounce one action off another in order to study the results.

Within our three-dimensional world, we pretend that there are consecutive moments, one following after the other like infinite automobiles rolling down a universal assembly line. This forces us to perceive action in a given sequence, even though it's a false picture that is portrayed to our physical senses. Indeed, past, present and future appear extremely convincing and logical when events seem to have lapses between them.

In the greater scope of the universal picture, however, all time is happening at once, or simultaneously. Our inner selves live in a spacious present unconstrained by time. When they view us pinpointed in time, they not only see our present self and situation, they see all the possibilities and probabilities that can ever occur to us, and all the ramifications—and they see this for our past, present and future. In other words, our inner selves see a field of probabilities that reflects every action, however minute, that we could possibly choose to actualize in physical reality. To them, linear time is meaningless.

The truth is, the moment that we are aware of right now is neither built from the past nor leads to the future, automatically flowing from one to the other. In this very moment we select events that we will call past, and we select events we will experience in the future; and in our next moment we select events that we will call past, and we select events we will experience in the future; et cetera, et cetera, et cetera, throughout physical life. Each moment is free to be defined exactly as we wish to see it, and that definition holds our perception of the past and future. Since all events occur at once in actuality, a past event cannot cause a present experience, and neither can cause a future one.

And, to reinforce that idea, here is a great Seth quote: "There is no cause and effect in the terms in which you understand the words. Nor is there a succession of moments that follow one after the other. And without a succession of moments following one after another, you can see that the idea of cause and effect becomes meaningless. An action in the present cannot be caused by an action in the past, and neither action can be the cause of future action, in a basic reality where neither past nor future exists."[4]

While this may sound esoteric, there are some very practical issues with simultaneous time that we need to understand, and one is that with no successive moments following one after the other, every probable event we can ever encounter must be surrounding us right now. For if all time is happening at once, then all possible events, or probabilities, must also be happening at once. And they are. Each probability is as solid as the next, already formed as a pattern in consciousness just awaiting our nod of approval to become part of our physical life. *And that includes placement into our past.* New events can be and are constantly selected from the great field of probabilities and inserted throughout linear time, so no matter where we perceive ourselves on the timeline, new events "happen" all around us, constantly.

Framework 2

Each of our lives is the result of a multidimensional creative venture. Our self in physical time works very closely with our self in nontime to pull it all off. Since our physical self is hampered by the assumptions of time and space and has a limited scope of conscious knowledge at its fingertips, the main work of creatively building a life, and all the events and material objects that entails, is done from what Seth calls Framework 2.

Framework 2 is a psychological medium, a place where our inner selves gather to do the work of keeping our reality in place.

Beware of the word "gather." Don't take it literally to mean our inner selves come from all over the universe to one spot designated by All That Is as the workplace. There are no levels, divisions, hierarchies or realms in the universal structure. Everything happens in consciousness through telepathic communication.

Of course, that applies to our objectified world, also. There really is no physical world set apart from consciousness. It's created within a different psychological medium, and there it continually resides. We translate the symbols of the medium into what seems to be solid structure, but as Seth says, there really are no walls to our house. They, like everything else in physical reality, are only "solid" because our perceptive mechanisms insist on making them seem that way. This psychological medium, physical reality, Seth calls Framework 1.

These framework designations are used for our benefit to help us grasp the bigger picture, but all areas of activity overlap each other in consciousness. In other words, Framework 1 and Framework 2 are in the same "place," sharing the same "space." However, from Framework 2's reality emerges physical reality. It is thought into existence by our collective inner selves based on instructions given them via our thoughts, attitudes, emotions and beliefs. And since each individual is an indivisible part of a personal inner self, it's accurate to say we each have a hand in the materialization of physical reality. In fact, Seth says that our world was actually created by us in that wider aspect of our existence.

Because it is the source of our world, Framework 2 contains not only all the knowledge it takes to build and maintain a physical reality and its creatures, it holds the information of all past, present and future events and other activity outside physical reality's boundaries. The probabilities that we have activated or one day will experience are already known as working models in Framework 2, as are the probabilities for every other consciousness who has or will exist on earth.

Thanks to our direct link to our inner self, and our "visits" to

Framework 2 in our dreams and those times when we're out of body, we know it intimately. We literally select the events we will insert into our life after studying our options. Our inner self guides us in our selections, but we're the ones who call the shots. There is not a moment of experienced life in which we have not chosen to participate.

Magnificence Personified

Nothing is as cut and dried in the universe as what I've written so far makes it seem. According to Seth, our minds can't study the whole picture because we must go beyond words to do so. Intuition, he says, will fill in the gaps that words can't interpret if we will but relax with it. But one thing that words can convey is this: We are magnificent creations of All That Is, with tremendous power at our fingertips. As literal parts of It, we share its propensities, desires and abilities, albeit in scaled-down versions.

There is stunning purpose to our being. All That Is *wanted* us. It loved us enough to give us life free of It's own, yet still remain a part of It. Along with the gift of existence came the ability to create. Everything in the universe creates the same way, be it All That Is, our greater selves, other energy gestalts or human beings. We, consciousness that we all are, do it by using our minds to think thoughts that eventually develop into psychological events. In the case of consciousness residing in a physical reality, those events may be interpreted as material objects, linear time experiences, dreams or psychic events.

Because telepathy is the mode of communication between and within consciousness, we are telepathic. Because consciousness units are clairvoyant and precognitive, we are also. Because each consciousness unit holds the history and knowledge of the universe, we're very well educated. Because consciousness is endowed with unpredictability, we have free will. Because consciousness creates every probability it can possibly experience, we are surrounded by potential unlimited. Because consciousness creates the camouflage of linear time, consciousness can choose to rethink its position and, instead, use the present as its continual point of power.

We are actors in a vast drama where the main action occurs outside our world. We can only sense the greater story from our perch in physicality, but realizing the activity that goes on within Framework 2 gives us a broader understanding of daily life. For, knowing what we do, can we possibly believe that an event can happen to us that doesn't have intent and meaning behind it, or why else would it have been formed and inserted into our reality? Can we really believe there is no purpose to the unfoldment of our lives? And can we see the great creativity at play that hands us, carte blanche, the means to build our lives as different from other people's as we choose, with no lockstep needed or wanted?

Consciousness is imbued with the desire to create, and that's what we do every moment of our lives. We can no more not create than the day not dawn. We do it unconsciously, consistently. The key to getting what we want out of life is, of course, to learn how to consciously create what we desire as individuals and as a world community.

Exploring Conscious Creation

Conscious creation is learning that consciousness is the building material from which we, little gods that we are, create terror and tragedy, just as it's the building material from which we create love sonnets and loving relationships. It's also learning that we can mold consciousness into whatever we choose; it does us the honor of becoming exactly what we will allow it to be.

Meshing the concepts of consciousness, simultaneous time, probabilities, and the creative aspects of thought, establishes the power platform of conscious creation. They are what, viewed as a whole, help us move toward the complete reorientation that will lead us into a clearer, more accurate understanding of physical reality and our participation in it. The power platform shows us the incredible flexibility of time, space and matter, and by so doing points the way to successful lives based on conscious choice. It eventually leads to that critical 180-degree evolution in our thinking, thank God.

So, for the rest of *Ten Thousand Whispers* we'll explore conscious creation in all of its glory, paying close attention to how and why an event is manifested, consciously or unconsciously. We'll start with discussion of key subjects laced with stories that have extraordinary implications, and then flow into a series of visualizations and techniques meant to help you use your power of thought, and the power of the moment, to consciously paint a living picture of your life, scene by scene.

As we mix and match our way through this fascinating subject, watch how your thinking changes. Keep an inner finger on the evolution of your beliefs, because as your beliefs change, so do you. By the time you reach the last chapter and last page, you'll be fully prepared to look life in the eye on your terms, tell it who's boss and move into your future with new assurance.

Ah, the beauty of it all.

2

...You are far more than the conscious mind, and the self which you do not admit is the portion that not only insures your own physical survival in the physical universe which it has made, but which is also the connective between yourself and inner reality ...It is only through the recognition of the inner self that the race of man will ever use its potential.
—Seth, **Seth, Dreams and Projection of Consciousness,**
Chapter 8

Calling Home

According to Seth, each of us is a multidimensional personality alive in numerous contexts both in and out of linear time. Physical reality isn't our only immediate place of residence; we reside in nontime, also. When we're in the dream state, for instance, we're literally outside time and space, pursuing our learning with the same fervor as when we're supposedly awake. We're also in nontime about fifty percent of the time we think we're really in physical reality. It seems we—hold on to your metaphysical hats—blink on and off constantly, spending some of the off-time with our inner selves in Framework 2, deciding which probabilities to pursue in the next moment and beyond.

Since there is only the spacious present, all of our past, future and "reincarnational" selves are as alive as we are today, experiencing their physical realities as clearly and as focused as ours is to us. So are all the probable selves we can ever become. Most of them live full and complete lives of their own, experiencing what we choose not to—or us experiencing what they choose not to, depending on how you look at it. What ties us all together? The fact that we are of the same consciousness, facets of our shared greater self feeding individual experience into the whole for contemplation and understanding.

Most of the subject of our multidimensionality has nothing to do with conscious creation, and, therefore, won't be discussed. Seth does a magnificent and extensive job of it in his books, and hearing it directly from the maestro of metaphysics is quite an experience. But there are several important issues that have everything to do with conscious creation, and can only be understood if the self is seen as extending beyond physical boundaries. These issues include the conscious activation of probable selves, event selections made in Framework 2 and our communication with our inner selves through the inner senses. The last one is the primary subject of this chapter, and the other two will be covered later.

First, remember that the units of consciousness (CUs) that form our inner selves, and us by extension, are both outside and inside physical reality at the same time. In fact, it's the CU's dual residency that allows us to be multidimensional. Since CUs communicate with each other constantly, no matter whether their address is Planet Earth or General Delivery: The Universe, logically it must mean there is a vehicle established to facilitate that back-and-forth communication. Ideas and perceptions do not float through the air on gossamer wings or on twinkling puffs of angels' breath. They travel a definite route established way back when and still in excellent operating order. As discussed in chapter one, that route is via the inner senses.

All needed material is delivered to the outer world from the inner world through the inner senses. Any information that reaches our conscious and subconscious mind from our inner self flows over the byways of the inner senses. It is through the inner senses that we experience intuition, impulses, inspiration, guidance, visions, the inner voice, etc., and even the more robust manifestations of communication such as channeling and automatic writing.

Why are the inner senses important to conscious creation? Because they carry the voice of our inner self. Through the inner senses we get feedback on what objectives to pursue in life, where we stand with the creation of those objectives and assistance in reaching them. The universe has created a way for us to be handed information of any sort when it's needed, wanted or thought to be helpful, but it takes a belief that the inner senses are real before we can consciously utilize the great storehouse of knowledge and assistance that flows through them into our minds and lives.

The best news we can know as human beings seemingly cut off from our source is that we're not. Each of us is in constant touch with our inner self through the inner senses, whether we believe it or not. In fact, it's just that, our belief or non-belief, that allows the communication to flow either unimpeded or blocked from them to us. The information we transmit to them has no barrier: It follows our thoughts, emotions and focus, and they pick it up loud and clear.

Through the inner senses our inner self prods us to enter the singing contest and gives us the encouragement we need to see it through. It suggests we phone the landlord of the building next door about the For Rent sign, and then helps us create the money to pay for our new apartment. It guides us into the probability where we lock eyes with a stranger destined to become the love of our life. So, the little dears, the inner senses, should be cultivated by us, patted and petted and fed bonbons. They are very, very important because if we don't accept them as real, they fade into the background of conscious thought, taking along with them our ability to consciously hear our inner self's guidance.

Ties that Bind

Perhaps the first desire that people new to metaphysics feel is a wish to experience some form of direct, knowing contact with "the universe." Since metaphysics is a broad term with as many points of view as people, there is no specifically-named presence to engage in conversation. Some use terminology such as Higher Self, whole self, higher power, Goddess, Universal Light, etc. It doesn't matter one whit what name is applied to our source. Our requests do not fall on deaf cosmic ears because we choose an improper salutation.

In this free-for-all called metaphysics, it is our universe bestowed right to build a thought system, or set of beliefs, around any subject of choice, and that includes our method of communicating with our inner self. If we read of someone who meditates for two hours a day and has great success in accomplishing his or her goal, whatever it may be, then we may think he or she has found "The Answer."

Ah, but next week we read of another person who swears the only way to contact a higher self is to face north, burn incense and chant monosyllables for twenty minutes every other day, and we wonder if maybe that's The Answer. As it turns out, The Answer is as individual as the individual, and it changes as he or she changes. Today's method is tomorrow's discard. Like everything else in physical reality, what we believe will work, does.

Communication between an individual and his or her inner self is the most natural thing in the universe, happening on a moment-by-moment basis; and one commonly held belief that has no validity whatsoever is that we must be in an altered state of consciousness to hear the conversation. The ways and means used by the inner self to get our attention are significant, and most of the time we're nowhere near a prayer bell when the event occurs. But it's still fun and rewarding to make contact through conscious efforts. After all, if we have an inner self, and if it is a thinking, experiencing energy gestalt, then what's to stop us from consciously communicating with it? Nothing but our belief in the impossibility of it all.

When I first read of Jane Roberts' and Robert Butts' discussions with Seth on the Ouija board, I thought, yeah, sure they talk through a moving pointer to this supposed greater portion of themselves residing outside space/time. Yeah, sure. Cynicism had always been my ace in the hole, the one position of substance that kept me solid and "rational." It also kept me from communicating directly with my inner self for years, even though I meditated almost every day and asked for such interaction. It simply didn't seem possible. Not that I doubted Jane and Rob once I came to trust their integrity. It was just that they were different or special or attuned or advanced...or something I wasn't.

Off We Go Into the Wild Yonder

But Stan and I brewed broader plans for ourselves in Framework 2, and God knows why, but we finally let an event enter the physical world that radically changed our lives. It was the fall of 1991 and we were at our home on an island in the Columbia River in Washington. Our main house in those days was in Eugene, Oregon, but we'd visit the island as often as possible.

One day before heading north to Washington, I came across an old Ouija board in our storage area that must have belonged to my children years previously. The weather had been thunderous in the Northwest for a day or two, and it crossed my mind that it might be fun to spend a rainy evening in front of the wood stove with a hot toddy and the Ouija board, listening to the soothing sounds of the river. An evening's entertainment, I thought. An understatement, I came to think.

As soon as Stan and I placed our fingers on the planchette it started whizzing around the board, spelling words so fast we could barely keep up. I was amazed and delighted; Stan yawned. No plans were made to continue the conversation beyond the evening; it still felt like a game. But, there we were, back at the board a week later, me with a list of questions, the Ouija board with answers to each and Stan still yawning. Eventually we came to know we were dealing with our combined inner selves, and we arbitrarily (or so we thought) started calling them the Committee.

Now, four years later, Stan and I can see what an intriguing phenomenon we've exposed ourselves to. First, Stan's interaction with the Committee actually started in 1984 while I was still a marketing manager with Apple Computer and he was a regional director for Wang Labs. I had just started reading the Seth material, and he was assiduously ignoring my efforts to have him do the same. Several times he mentioned that he was "picking up on something from some committee or something" that was telling him stuff about me, things such as some day I'd be teaching the same material I was now reading.

I almost choked in disbelief and frustration. Not only was I unsure of my own stand with metaphysics, I damn well wasn't going to impact my career with such nonconformity. And furthermore, he could stop playing games because I wasn't buying it—oh, sure he was "hearing voices." And so he did indeed stop. After a few times of tolerating my rolling eyes, he said he'd not tell me anything else they said. He didn't, and they went away. We both forgot the incident until long after we'd decided to call the energy behind the planchette the Committee.

Now we talk to them maybe once a week, I with anticipation, Stan with resignation. For all his foot-dragging, it's become apparent that he's the main conduit for the energy that gets funneled onto the board. Stan can sit down with anyone at the Ouija board—which he won't do often and seldom without cajoling— and the planchette takes off. I try it with others and we get a good response to yes/no questions, but not much else.

Messages From Beyond

It's really quite fascinating, this talking to "energy gestalts" who intimately know every thought, word and deed of ours since birth. One day I said, "You really know every thought we think?" And they said, "Yes, it's easy. But don't worry...we're discreet." They know every feeling, too. Once we were discussing a subject that had emotional ramifications for me, and I felt the instant build-up of feeling over something under discussion. The pointer paused for a moment, and then the Committee said, "Upset, are we?"

That kind of thing happens often, that interplay between all of us. Our conversations on the board are just that—interactive conversations. The Committee doesn't spell everything out; either Stan or I pick up on sentences, phrases or paragraphs before they're worded, we'll say them and the Committee will flash to "yes" for verification or continue with the spelling if the answer is no. The conversations move almost as quickly as ones with our physical friends, and they're just as loaded with jokes, seriousness, prodding and caring. "Geez" is what they call Stan. It's short for Old Geezer. They say he's been around long enough to warrant the title, and they're not just talking about this lifetime.

The Committee has suggested several words be written on the board for speed, ones that they use frequently. In fact, one day they asked Stan to get a pen and bring it to the board. He returned with a magic marker and ballpoint pen. Without identifying their types, he said, "Which do you want?" They replied, "The magic marker. Now, write the word 'sure' on the board."

Just in this last year their awareness of our exterior environment has become more obvious. One day before starting a session, Stan, an amateur photographer, set his camera for some hopeful shots of island deer. Before joining me at the board for our session, he jokingly said, while standing at the front door searching the river grass for movement, "Okay, Committee, let me know when deer show up." Then he sat down out of sight of the door and we commenced with our questions. About ten minutes later, in mid-sentence, the Committee interrupted with, "There are your deer, Geez." Sure enough, when Stan got to the door for a clear view of the field, two Bambis stood looking our way.

We always tape record our sessions, and sometimes it's done in a sound studio in our home. Stan, the audio technician of the family, uses a microphone attached to a boom arm that moves up and down for positioning purposes. I usually settle in before a Ouija session with a cup of tea and my list of questions, and this time was no different. I placed both items on the table next to my elbow, the same one that held the boom arm pushed back out of the way. About fifteen minutes after the session started, the Committee said to me, "You'd better move your tea. The microphone is about to topple into it." Sure enough, the boom arm had loosened and the mike was sinking slowly toward the table, hovering about two inches above the rim of my teacup by the time I caught it.

Another time we had been worried about the mother cat of the newborn kittens born on our property. Ginger Peachie hadn't been seen around her babies for the better part of a day, and our concern for her and the kittens was growing. That afternoon Stan and I sat down for a Ouija session, but never brought the subject up with the Committee.

About twenty minutes into our conversation, they stopped what they were saying and inserted, "Ginger's back." Stan said, "Mind if I go take a look?" They said, sure, go ahead, so outside he went, walking around the deck, past the wood pile and out into the blackberry bushes where the kittens were temporarily living. Ginger was lazily feeding her babies, oblivious to our concern. Stan returned to the Ouija board and said, "Yes, she's returned." And the Committee replied, "What did you expect—Thomas?"

Nothing's Sacred

It's rather startling when the realization dawns that something, somewhere knows your every move. It's not uncommon for the Committee to comment on Stan's and my off-the-board conversations or experiences. One time we had stopped at an historic Oregon inn for dinner on our way home from California. The food was so-so, but we had an intriguing discussion. Days later the Committee said, "We liked the ambiance of the inn, and the conversation was great, but the Chicken Cordon Bleu was as tough as rubber."

Another time, I had been visualizing while out on a walk along the river. I mentioned the subject of my visualization to the Committee the next time we were on the Ouija board, and they said, "No, that's not all you were visualizing." I argued the point until they suggested Stan and I go out to dinner and think about it. About half way into the meal, it hit me. They were absolutely right, I had been visualizing a second goal that had completely slipped my mind.

According to the Committee, the information we receive on the board comes through our inner senses. But they're very adamant that all the insights and assistance they give are available through the inner senses off the board, also. In fact, they say that intuition, insight, impulses and the inner voice are the natural, normal channels for communication and should be developed fully for a truly balanced life. At times they don't give us answers to specific questions, but instead suggest we listen to our inner voices. Then, when we go back to the board to report what we've heard, they'll verify whether it was indeed what was communicated and whether it was colored by our belief systems.

Lately our communication with the Committee has taken an intriguing turn we never could have anticipated, if communication is what it can be called. Things happen off the board that have no seemingly direct connection with them, but... Like the time I was searching my mind for the name of the commonly known Italian ice cream. I was sitting in the living room after dinner one night talking to Stan across the room. It was a quiet winter evening. The house was snugly bundled up from the outside cold, and you could hear a pin drop.

I said aloud, getting a kick out of it, "Hey Committee, what's the word I'm looking for?" After a few moments more of searching my mind, it clicked. "Spumoni!" I yelled. I no sooner let the word fly than we very distinctly heard in the room the clear note of a bell pealing three times, as though to say, "Bingo!" When I brought it up later on the board all the Committee would say was, "Heh heh."

But the most dramatic event actually happened twice. Stan called me in Eugene from Washington one day and our conversation evolved into a discussion of the Committee, only this time our talk was quite hilarious. Stan and the Committee have a running joke about them being, in Stan's words, "little green trolls under the bridge," at which they pretend to take umbrage, and he had launched into a dialogue quite pointed and funny. As we were wrapping up our last chuckle, Stan said, "If this phone line goes dead, I'll know I'm in trouble." Instantly the phones were disconnected.

Then a month or so later we were on the phone again, I in Washington this time and Stan in Eugene. Stan was urging me to remember to take the advice the Committee had offered in response to a dilemma I was facing, but I wasn't in the mood to listen. Rather flippantly I said, "The Committee can go to hell." Stan quickly replied, "Honey, don't do it!" And the phone line went dead. Later, over the Ouija board, they started the day's discussion with, "If you tell us to go to hell one more time, we will inflate your phone bill by a factor of ten."

Pretty funny, but then in all seriousness they continued, "You two did it both times. You chose the events you wanted to experience and then put them into place. Whose reality is it, gang?" I said, "Okay, but you actually created them, right? You made the events happen."

"Well," they said, "we is you." Go figure.

Cosmic Sidekicks

My point in telling you about the Committee has a definite purpose. It's to help broaden your view, if needed or wanted, of what an inner self is and is not. Stan and I became convinced we were communicating with our inner selves. That conviction led us to reassess our interpretation, or definition, of an inner self because it opened our minds to possibilities never previously entertained. We've come to realize that an inner self is not detached ethereal energy that deals in abstracts. It's not elusive, it's not just something we sense, it's not a computer-like being that simply processes information and it's not a deity to be worshipped.

Inner selves are as alive and vital as each of us; in fact, we are a portion of them, emerging into physical reality with them at our side and as close as our minds. They have personality, character and humor. They don't use the camouflage of matter to create a noticeable body for themselves, but nonetheless they are whole and complete. They are energy gestalts with a life of their own and a job to do—but, then, so are we.

You can take my word for it or find out for yourself, but your inner self is no different from our Committee. Maybe it is a little less intrusive into physical reality, but that's all—and you may be able to make that difference a temporary one. I can't stress strongly enough that your inner self hears your every thought and word, senses your every emotion and feeling. It has to, since that's how it knows what to create in your reality.

It wants the best for you, does everything it can to help you out, cares deeply for you. You don't have to do anything special to get your inner self's attention. All you have to do is talk to it. Standing at a bus corner, sitting in deep meditation, watching a blazing sunset, it simply doesn't matter. It hears your thoughts and responds to your needs. The issue is whether or not you hear its response. One day I was in emotional turmoil and I asked the Committee to tell me what to do. Nothing "came through." Later, over the board, I asked if they'd heard my request. They said, of course they had, but my emotion blocked my ability to get what they were sending.

See how it goes? It's up to us to make the communication work. Our inner selves do their job, and it's up to us to do ours. What I desire more than anything is to flow through life with ease, with no blocks of any significance in my way. Knowing it's possible, because I believe what Seth says, means all I need do is learn how to do it. One piece of the puzzle, albeit a very important one, is to hear more fully the guidance that can take me where I want to go, effortlessly. Same for you.

Hearing our guidance doesn't necessarily mean a news bulletin is broadcast across the screen of our mind. Oh, if only that were the case, but it's usually more subtle: the flitting thought suggesting an immediate course of action be undertaken, the light bulb that illuminates a new idea, the sense that something is amiss, the feeling that everything is under control. Remember, your inner self extends itself into your reality via the inner senses and shares your conscious mind, so naturally it uses your mind to communicate data.

One time I picked up the phone to dial Stan, and there he was, already on the line and wondering how I knew he was calling since the phone hadn't rung. Another time I was walking by our front door and on impulse opened it. Perched on the porch was one of our kittens, patiently awaiting the removal of the barricade that kept her from the comfort of the couch pillows. These types of events happen to all of us all the time. Gee, what coincidences. Or are they updates from our inner selves about our psychic environments?

One day the same little kitten seemed ill. After reviewing her symptoms with the veterinarian, she strongly suggested I bring Missy Motley to the office, saying that what I'd described sounded life-threatening. Knowing many probabilities surrounded the event, I dragged my feet. Missy Motley could barely stand, but she seemed to want to join her brothers outside on the grass. I let her go, poised to rush to her side if needed.

I was pressed for time. The car was packed and I was about to close the house for three days while I journeyed south to meet Stan on business. I couldn't decide what to do about Missy, so I stood quietly and asked for guidance. The kitten made a feeble attempt to romp and play, but finally decided to curl up close by her frisky brothers and soak in the sun.

Then an interesting thing happened in the blink of an eyelash. I simply knew she was going to be fine. I've never felt so sure about the outcome of anything so potentially serious. I knew that I could drive away for three days and come back to a healthy baby. I never gave the probability of her dying or being hopelessly sick another thought. When I returned home, there she was, bouncing across the river sand at my call.

I love that little creature. She and I share a definite bond. So how I came to leave her home sick for three days challenges the rational mind. But once I made the decision to leave her, I felt free, like a very significant event had just occurred. In talking to the Committee later, I confirmed that, with their assistance, I had sensed (inner sensed?) the strongest probability surrounding the situation and allowed it to be played out in time without interference. I could have selected a different probability, if Missy had gone along with it, where she could have died. But neither of us put our energy behind making it happen, and so it dissipated into a non-event.

Catching Probabilities on the Fly

Speaking of probabilities and guidance, here's a story with an interesting slant on both of them. I was driving south from Washington to our Oregon home one fine day. Since Stan and I make the four-hour ride regularly, I knew the interstate highway had been under repair for over a month. The week before I had been delayed forty-five minutes, and I didn't want to face that again. For many months I'd been practicing hearing the Committee in my thoughts and I was becoming quite good at distinguishing their words from my own. I could ask a question of them, and under most circumstances hear their answer.

About seventy miles north of the point of repair, I asked the Committee if the highway was clear that day. No, it was blocked, they said. Okay, I thought, that means I'll detour into the country and come into Eugene the back way, only adding fifteen minutes to my drive instead of nearly an hour spent frozen on a standstill freeway. When I reached the point of my detour, which was maybe five miles north of the repair area, I turned off and stopped at a mini-market to get a soda. On impulse I asked the clerk if she knew whether or not the highway was blocked. She said she didn't think so, because none of the truckers had mentioned any problems.

Now I'm in a dilemma. If I'd heard right, the Committee had said there was a pile up; this woman thought not. I climbed into my car and proceeded to ask the Committee once more about the status of the road. This time I heard it was clear. Terrific, now what do I do? Which time had I accurately heard the Committee? And, more practically, what should I do about getting home? I chose the main highway and sailed into Eugene with no problem.

On the Ouija board that night I asked if I'd first heard correctly that the highway was closed. Yes, they said, you did. Well, then did I hear seventy miles later that the highway was open? Yes, they said, you did. How can that be, I asked? It doesn't make sense. The Committee said, "You're about to use logic again to try to figure this out, when the answer is not logical in your terms. What happened was that you changed probabilities. You relaxed after you heard us the first time, you dropped your concern and moved your thoughts on to other subjects. *You allowed another probability to enter the picture.*"

Maybe what's just as fascinating is what they said next. "The real learning in this situation isn't whether or not you heard us correctly. It is in the fact that you followed an *impulse* and asked the clerk her opinion. By so doing, you brought new data into your conscious awareness that was meant to assist you in making your decision. Asking us constantly for direction isn't the way to move through life because we'd have to keep an obvious running dialogue active every moment, and that's not practical since it means you would have to be consciously aware of us at all times. Our normal communication vehicle with you is through impulse and intuition."

Our inner selves don't wait for us to query them for guidance; they offer it every second of our lives. Impulses, Seth says, are the closest communication that we experience with our inner self. They are spontaneous urgings toward action, and if our beliefs don't get in the way, they lead us on a path of fulfillment. They head us toward our goals and away from pain; they lead us to the one we love and out of a bad relationship; they help us find the butter in the new supermarket and a place to store household items. Impulses, more than anything else, show us how caring our inner selves are, because they are the results of quick assessment and suggestions for action by the energy that forms us and our environment.

Mirror, Mirror

Another method of direct communication with our inner self takes place as what we term telepathy. They send us mind pictures or words that flash information on the bulletin board of our innards. At times we don't consciously recognize the news flash as anything other than a stray thought from nowhere; we don't see or sense the tie-in to the great communication highway between the inner and outer world.

As I went about my daily chores one day, a thought came to mind which I had never previously entertained. I wondered what it would be like to be blind, and if the blind could feel or sense color. Not five minutes later, my actress daughter called in great excitement. She'd just landed the lead in a play about a blind girl with heightened sensitivity to her environment.

While studying an upcoming projects list another time, my eyes settled on one in particular. It was a radio show on which I wanted to be interviewed, and it was on my list because I needed to mail them a copy of my first book, *Beyond the Winning Streak*. I remembered that Stan had some information for me regarding the show, so I placed a call to his beeper.

Within seconds my phone rang. It was Stan. I said, "That was a fast response." He didn't know what I was talking about; he said he'd had a thought about the radio show that he wanted to pass on to me, so he'd called. Just when he finished his sentence, his beeper rang with my message.

One of the most startling episodes of telepathy I experienced happened long before my introduction to metaphysics. Newly divorced, I moved my two small children into an apartment complex. My six-year-old son asked if he could take his one-year-old sister by the hand and walk her around our building. Since I was in the midst of unpacking, it sounded like a great idea, so I sent them on their way with an admonition to be careful. About five minutes later, I was in the bathroom unloading makeup into a drawer when I happened to glance into the mirror. My mind blanked and I "saw" the gate to the pool wide open and Matt grabbing Cathleen's hand and jerking her away from the water's edge. No other people were in the scene.

I ran out of the apartment and frantically searched for the pool. I'd not previously perused the grounds so I had no conscious idea of where it was located, but I quickly found myself standing at the open pool gate. The kids were nowhere to be found in the vacant swimming area. I headed back toward our apartment shouting their names, and finally heard Matt's return call. He hurried toward me, obviously upset, dragging his sister by the hand. It seems he had taken Cathleen for a walk at the water's edge, and she'd slipped. Just in the nick of time Matt had tightened his grip on her little hand and pulled her back to safety.

Setting the Stage for Whispers

Hearing our inner guidance isn't usually that dramatic. More likely it's quiet assistance that we don't even know we've received. We react in a certain way and don't question why. Not that we need to, as long as we go where we want to go. It's when we block or intellectualize the information coming through our inner senses that problems arise. That's when we rethink an impulse and don't call our aged aunt, only to learn later she was slipping into depression and our voice would have soothed. It's when we ignore the unease about marrying a certain person and end up in divorce court years later.

What I found extremely helpful in my early days of metaphysics, when I didn't have the slightest notion of how to interact consciously with my inner self, was to meditate. I don't do it as much now, but it was very important to me back then. What it did was to allow me to silence my mind and start building a belief that I could consciously hear my guidance. Not that I did, particularly, but I started believing it was possible. Later, after my confidence increased and I started sensing or hearing things in real time, I got away from lengthy meditations. I still use an altered state, or what Seth calls psychological time, or Psy-Time, frequently to visualize future events and work with beliefs, but I seldom meditate with the express purpose of gaining insights.

That's not to say I've found The Answer. I have for me, but not necessarily for you—and mine probably will change over the years. As individualized consciousness in physical form, there can't possibly be one designated path that, when uncovered, leads all explorers into ultimate fulfillment. We're so creative, and so different in make-up from our fellow travelers, that we'll approach our psychic growth from any number of angles, trying this and that and shedding it when it no longer applies.

In my more naive days, when I thought my answer was everyone's, I asked the Committee whether there was a need to go into a meditative state once we "grew beyond" it, thinking they'd say no...and pat me on the head for having uncovered a universal truth. Instead they said, "For some of you, yes, because individually you may have set things up that way. You create the needs, the rituals and the processes in order to accomplish what you will in your personal hallucination of physical reality." Individual flexibility is the name of the game in this fascinating world of fiction made fact.

So where's all the "spirituality" in this down-to-earth, practical, clear interaction with our inner selves? I guess it depends on your definition of spirituality, which, of course, is a reflection of your beliefs. If you want your inner self to be just this side of God, no problem. It will play the part beautifully, using thees and thous as freely as necessary to make you feel comfortable. If you want to pay homage to your inner self, assign it the role of deity in metaphysical clothing or visitor from another planet, that's fine, too. After all, it is your reality; you have a right, as consciousness in physicality learning to deal with idea constructions, to act on your beliefs of choice.

Just a friendly suggestion, take it or leave it. Try not to set your inner self too far apart from your natural being; don't see it as a pattern of perfection you must strive toward but which is ultimately beyond your grasp, or as a being light years ahead of you in spiritual growth. It's a long way back to reality when the trip starts so far from home, and as a race we've seen too many centuries of such detachment and its consequences to want to experience more. Enough must some day be enough.

3

...In your present moment of time, you are positioned in the center of a cosmic web of probabilities that is affected by your slightest mental or emotional act.

—*Seth,* The "Unknown" Reality, Volume One, *Session 686*

On a Moment's Notice

Understanding simultaneous time becomes an important factor in deciphering clues to conscious creation. It's a fascinating subject and one loaded with insights as to how the physical world is formed on a moment-by-moment basis. When we understand what we're dealing with, the flexibility of this reality becomes so apparent that we wonder why we didn't catch on to it more quickly.

Oversoul Seven and the Museum of Time is a delightful novel by Jane Roberts about Oversoul Seven, a nonphysical oversoul who has reached a certain level of education and expertise with the unknowing help of several of his aspects (souls) in physical reality, whom he instructs and assists. At one point, Cypress, Seven's oversoul and mentor, calls him to a meeting in Framework 2.

For educational purposes, Seven chooses not to remember that he has visited Framework 2 many times, and so is enchanted by the scene Cypress has created for him, an outdoor earth setting of great beauty. Seven says, "But everything looks brand new...as if it were all created in this instant. I mean, that one rose...It's a bud, so of *course* it looks new. But beside it is a much bigger rose, with all of its petals open and *it* looks brand-new too!" With an enigmatic smile Cypress replies, "Precisely."

From the words of this novel comes literal truth. According to Seth, every moment of experience is a "new" one, replete with newly formed physical objects that have entered this reality through the immediate moment point of time. Our moments are constantly refreshed from Framework 2, where everything is created anew before entering our lives.

The implication of that information boggles the mind. Nothing is in physical reality long enough to age! Not our bodies, not material objects, not nature. It's all created on a moment-by-moment basis under the watchful eyes and adept hands of our inner selves. Seth says, "No particular object 'exists long enough' as an indivisible, rigid, or identical thing to change with age. The energy behind it weakens. The physical pattern therefore blurs. After a certain point each re-creation becomes less perfect....After many such re-creations that have been unperceived by you, then you notice a difference and assume that a change...has occurred....Matter of itself, however, is no more continuous, no more given to growth or age, than is, say, the color yellow."[1]

Another mind-stretching implication of the simultaneous time/Framework 2 idea is that everything we see and experience in physical reality is *after the fact*. It's old news. Our thoughts, attitudes and beliefs suggest which events will be chosen from the infinite field of probabilities. Then, in the dream or out-of-body state, we try them on for size, and if they are acceptable to us (i.e., reflect the symbols of our beliefs and expectations precisely), in they come to physical reality. So what we *experience* in the present was started by previous thoughts and finished in Framework 2 prior to its appearance in our lives; what we *think* in the present starts the selection of the next event.

How surprised we are when we "happen" to meet an old friend unexpectedly. How enraged we are when passed over for promotion. How powerless we feel when we believe another's energy has impacted us negatively. How excited we are after a blind date that worked. How astonished we feel when we win the lottery. How frightened we are at an act of violence. How desolate we feel when our house burns down. How joyous we are at the birth of our baby.

The question on the table: Do you remember why any event can happen in the first place? Because we're consciousness here to learn that our thoughts have creative power, and our journey into physicality is specifically chosen so we can see our idea constructions in living color and determine their effects. We're here to play with energy and see what happens. That we experience events of horror or joy is neutral in the greater scheme of things. They are simply scenes reflective of our inner psychological makeup.

Obviously, they are not neutral when met in our lives, because in physicality we're dealing with feelings and emotions meant to warn us when our idea constructions are off kilter, or not to the good of ourselves or others. And that's why we're studying simultaneous time in the first place, to learn its flexibility and the ease it offers of changing what we don't like in our lives.

Selecting New Probabilities

Probabilities reside outside time and space, as do the controllers of those probabilities, our inner selves. In other words, the activity generated by our thoughts is handled outside physical reality where time and space have no validity, and therefore don't impact the selection of probabilities.

From our knowledge of simultaneous time and consciousness emerges an understanding as to how probabilities function. The ebb and flow of life is the result of the unpredictable nature of consciousness units. They can be what they want to be, when they want to be it. Never are they predestined by God or the universe to become part of an event or object. What directs them into certain molds is thought held in the present moment. That thought then nudges CUs toward probabilities that best reflect the meaning behind the thought. This applies to personal, individual events and mass events shared by many others. In no way can we predict what will happen to us for sure, because we can choose to accept as our reality any number of given unpredictable events at any time, right up to the last minute, so to speak.

So, can world or personal events be forecasted by seers and psychics? Absolutely. They are consciousness with clairvoyant and telepathic abilities, just like the rest of us. Their skills may be honed more sharply than ours, that's all. But what they pick up is only the most probable outcome based on the thoughts that are forming it *at the moment*. By changing thoughts, the event loses its intensity and becomes less of a probability. The new thoughts then activate other probabilities that start their movement toward actualization. Whether it's the thoughts of an individual or a large group of people, it works the same way.

What this tells us very clearly is reflected in one of Seth's most incredible statements: The point of power is in the present. He maintains that all events—past, present and future—are selected in the present moment based on our thoughts. Knowing this, he says, clears our eyes to the fact that we have inexhaustible energy and ability at our command, and it releases us from the psychological need to test ourselves against the barriers of the past. "...The point of power is in the present, and from that moment you choose which you, and which world."[2]

Now, doesn't this tell us something important? Something life changing? It tells us that there *is no past*. There is no past! We build a past in the present based on the probabilities to which we give the most intensity through our thoughts. It means the hurts, the sadness, the supposed failures no longer can derail our lives, unless we continue to reinforce them by our belief in them. We can set them on the back shelf of our memories, turn our present around with a change of attitude and beliefs, and get on with getting on.

This fact, more than any other, gives us back our freedom. Our past can no longer impact us, unless we allow it to. We, dear friends, are truly free spirits, with great power at our fingertips—the power to not only create our lives one time, but over and over and over again, based on new probability selections.

Each moment of our life is drenched in possibility, because each moment is drenched in probabilities. The selection of new probabilities doesn't happen just once a month; it happens constantly throughout the day. Each choice we make has within it the ability to get us to where we want to go, even if the decision seems "wrong" at the time. How can it not, when every probability we can ever encounter surrounds us right now? The great flexibility of our reality constantly allows for forward movement; we're never boxed into a corner with nowhere to go, even when it seems we've hit the proverbial wall.

Creation's Moment Point

"Will I ever get it?" I wondered for the thousandth time, with a twinge of desperation coloring the thought. "Will I ever have complete faith in my ability to allow the universe to support me? I mean, not just sometime, but all the time, no matter what?" I fell asleep with those words running through my mind, and awoke to pack for my trip to Virginia. I was on my way to spend the Fourth of July with my children. Matt and Cathleen were temporarily sharing housing in Fairfax while Cathleen was finishing her degree at a university blocks from their home. One of the last items to go into my suitcase was a new mystery I'd purchased the previous week. That night in bed I pulled the book out and, as the universe would have it, kicked off a whole summer of questions around the subject of simultaneous time.

The mystery was a humorous one about a group of nuns who

found themselves in the midst of drug dealers and worse. One of the nuns, the heroine of the story, was almost revered by her cohorts because she had what they called "perfect faith." They defined it as the unequivocal assumption that everything would always work out just fine, that there was no situation that wouldn't sort itself out to the holder's benefit, because God would protect her or him. And that's exactly what happened to our heroine time after time, as she raced between murderers and Mafia. She was not only sheltered from harm, she led the way to some very dramatic successes.

I was quite taken by the idea of perfect faith and what it represented. Setting aside the belief that it was an outside source protecting her, I still felt the nun was on to something. Yes, that's what I wanted, perfect faith. I mulled it over, thought about what the nun had faced and conquered, and even though it was fiction, I knew it didn't have to be. I knew perfect faith is what we all can feel, and that the outcome would be the same for us as for the book's heroine.

When I returned home, Stan and I talked to the Committee about perfect faith. They said that, in case I hadn't yet caught on, I should know it led the list of subjects I had chosen to learn this time around. While that statement in itself was thought-provoking, it took a back seat to the bombshell answer to my next question, which was—and don't ask me why I asked it or even how it entered my head to ask—"When was the material on perfect faith placed in that book?" Their answer: the night I needed assistance.

Now's the Time

I thought my subject to be learned that summer of 1993 was perfect faith, and indeed it was. But intertwined, because it's what makes the idea of perfect faith a functionally sound concept, was simultaneous time. When does creation happen? Now. When does a probability get selected from the infinite field of probabilities and inserted into our life? Now. And which thoughts, emotions, beliefs, attitudes and expectations select the next probability? The ones we hold...now. Everything happens in the spacious present. It is, as Seth says, the point of power. "The present as you think of it, and in practical working terms, is the point at which you select your physical experience from all those events that <u>could</u> be materialized."[3]

High on my list of favorite Seth quotes is the one I mentioned in "The 180-Degree Turn," and I'm going to repeat it here because of its breakthrough significance: "There is no cause and effect in the terms in which you understand the words. Nor is there a succession of moments that follow one after the other. And without a succession of moments following one after the other, you can see that the idea of cause and effect becomes meaningless. An action in the present cannot be caused by an action in the past, and neither action can be the cause of future action, in a basic reality where neither past nor future exist."[4]

Cause and effect, the theory that has the world mesmerized. Almost all plans of action, responses, attitudes, reactions, decisions and emotions are based on a belief in cause and effect. And if there is no such thing, what happens to our thinking? Just about everything, and all of it good. We become free to view events with a radical new eye and figure out just what the heck it is we're dealing with in physical reality.

I'd been back at the office for a few days after returning from Virginia when I opened the publication produced by a distributor of *Beyond the Winning Streak* and perused the pages for the ad we'd placed in that issue. I gave it a second flip-through, because the first time I hadn't found the ad. I didn't the second time, either. Damn! It was to have been the kick-off in our advertising efforts for the book. We'd finally gotten serious about marketing it, and look what happened, the ad was never run! Now we'd have to wait another two months and lose valuable time in the process.

Then the phrase "perfect faith" crept into my mind. Oh, yeah, I'm supposed to be learning this stuff, but this isn't the time to try.

After all, it's after the fact. The damage is already done. Well, what can it hurt? It sure beats getting angry, and maybe there's a silver lining I can't yet see—like, well...I can't think of one.

So I sat at my desk and closed my eyes. I calmed down, cleared my thoughts and said "perfect faith." I used that phrase as a signal to settle in, let it be, accept, know, release. I felt my mind clear and then visualized a short scene of me feeling very happy in this moment. I opened my eyes and smiled, knowing (or hoping I knew) it had worked. The whole process took maybe a minute.

I reached for the phone and called our distributor. "Oh, yes," our ad rep said, "you're right, the ad didn't run in the July issue. It ran in the special May/June issue that was circulated to twice the usual audience because it was handed out at the annual publishing convention that month. Although your artwork arrived after the cut-off date, we had space available and squeezed you in."

Okay, Committee, what happened? When was that ad placed in the May/June publication? According to them, it was the moment I decided to challenge the outcome of what looked like a dead end. Operating from the present, I opened up probabilities in the "past" and allowed a different ending to the story to occur.

A Future Self's Helping Hand

How about impacting the present from the future? Is that a possibility? If simultaneous time is valid, it must be. Here's a story for you; you can draw your own conclusions. One day I walked into a store for an unplanned shopping trip. As I went to pay for my $95 item, I found I had left my credit cards and check book at home. Then a memory flashed of Stan giving me $100 a week previously and of me placing it in my purse. I dug it out and paid for my purchase.

I started wondering about that money, since it's not common for Stan to hand me such a sum unless there is a reason. Mostly I wondered if I'd created the memory and the money in my moment of need. In talking to the Committee that night they said, no, that wasn't the case. It seems my future self had reached "back" in time to the previous week and, knowing I would need the money, prompted Stan to offer it to me. He complied, and I stuffed it away. The future self who helped me out was the "me" in the store desiring the $95 item.

Little Ol' Matter Generators

And then there was the question about a forgotten blue coat I suddenly remembered was tucked away in a storage container. I was headed to the East Coast in February and needed a dressy, ultra-warm coat. A couple years previously we'd moved from house to house and in the process had stored little-used items in a warehouse. Again I flashed on a memory, this time of the blue coat, so I drove to the storage area and dug it out. I was relieved to find it, because truthfully I couldn't quite remember if I really owned one or if it was a figment of my imagination.

By now I was learning to question seemingly innocuous events, ones we all meet every day in our realities, so I asked the Committee when exactly the blue coat was placed in the storage area— two years ago or the moment I thought of it. When I thought of it, they said. It seems I placed it in my memory at that point and as-signed it to the past.

As an intriguing aside, the Committee says that until we enter a room or view a scene—until we *experience* it—there is nothing materialized in our space continuum. It's all there as psychic, or psychological, patterns, but until we actualize them through one or more of our senses (meaning we see, feel, hear, taste or smell them), they are not solidified into matter. In fact, whatever scene is behind our heads at this very moment is not materialized in our private physical reality until we experience it in some sensory way. We're all constant little matter generators, it seems.

In the Blink of an Eye

How fast can we change our reality? As fast as we can change our thoughts, attitudes, beliefs, focus or intent. Probabilities always surround us, and we select the ones to be activated in physical reality as each moment progresses. According to Seth, we change probabilities constantly and, using his word, seamlessly. As we become more aware of the flow of probabilities in and out of our days, there comes a time when we can almost spot the seam.

The first time I spaced out Portland, I not only didn't spot the seam, I tried to convince myself there wasn't any. Stan and I had just moved to the Northwest that year, and I wasn't very familiar with the drive between our home in Oregon and the house we'd just purchased on the island in Washington. It's a two-hundred-mile trip between the two and the scenery is lovely, but cruising through Portland is special. From the freeway bridges high above the city, the view is of skyscrapers and emerald green parks nestled up to the gracious Willamette River.

On this particular trip I was headed north from Eugene. Then, at the southernmost border of Portland, a strange thing happened. One moment I had yet to reach the city; the next, I was five miles *north* of the downtown area. To set the record straight, I was completely sober, in a great frame of mind, playing "Chariots of Fire" on the tape deck and looking forward to seeing Portland on this clear, gorgeous day.

When I reached the island hours later, I dug out a map of the city and scanned it for clues that would tell me I'd made a mistake, that I'd simply taken a bypass, a more direct route in error, or something.... I would have accepted any small morsel of "fact" that suggested nothing unusual had occurred. No matter how I analyzed the map, the conclusion I was forced to draw was that I had hit a blip on the space/time line. And the oddity didn't stop there. I called Stan back in Eugene and exclaimed, "You'll never guess what happened when I got to Portland!" His immediate response, "The city disappeared."

Ah, but five years later when it happened again, I was much

more prepared to understand. We'd been talking to the Committee for almost four years at that point, and with many odd events now under my belt, I took this one at face value immediately. I'd spent the day in Lake Oswego, a southern suburb of Portland, at Bettie Kielty's home planning Seth Network International's next big conference with her and Nancy Walker. Stan had been delayed that day in Eugene, so he missed the ride through hyperspace.

Nancy, Bettie and I had gone to a local restaurant for a late dinner and then I headed north to the island. With a soft rain beating on the windows, I settled in for a quiet, cozy drive home. About three minutes or so after I entered the freeway, it crossed my mind to stay in the right lanes so I'd be positioned to continue on Interstate 5 through Portland instead of being forced at an upcoming fork in the road onto another highway heading west. Based on the familiar exterior scene rolling by, I figured I was maybe five miles from the fork.

Less than a minute later I noticed the next exit sign begin to appear down the road. I kept my eyes on it as it approached, interested in checking my exact location. I didn't spot the seam because it was so smooth, but in that minute or so of time I had traveled over ten miles and once again missed the city. The exit sign I viewed was almost at the Washington/Oregon border, on the far side of Portland.

Materializing Luggage

"Sorry, folks, it looks like all your luggage was left at the Portland airport in error," said the United Airlines representative at the baggage carousel at San Francisco International Airport. After much moaning and groaning, about twenty Portland passengers, including Stan and me, were led to a special table set up to handle lost luggage claims for our group.

No, I thought, this is only one probability. We don't have to accept it, at least not without giving it a fight. So I relaxed, thought of the various probabilities around the situation and saw us walking away with our luggage. Stan was doing the same, although without consciously deciding to alter probabilities. Then came a phone call to the harried airline representative. All the luggage had made it to San Francisco, but had been unloaded in an incorrect building, he was told—a mistake no one could fathom.

Later, in response to a question, the Committee said the bags had been materialized in our reality while we were filling out the lost luggage forms, meaning we had indeed changed probabilities.

A Kitten Moves On

Humans are not the only ones who select probabilities, consciously or otherwise. Every form of consciousness goes through the same process, at some level making decisions about what it chooses to experience. An interesting event occurred with a little gray kitten that brought home that fact.

One of our cats, Blackie, had given birth to five kittens across the road in an abandoned shack. It was a joy to watch her lead them up our driveway one sunny day, bringing her young home for the first time. Stan and I watched in delight as they progressed toward their new living quarters, which seemed to be our garage, since that's the direction in which Blackie was headed.

About halfway through their trip, one little gray kitten veered off into some tall weeds by the side of the driveway that led to heavier undergrowth. Since another cat went with it, seemingly to overlook its side excursion, we didn't worry. But as the minutes passed, Stan and I decided enough was enough. We'd go find the kitten and bring it to its mother. We searched the weeds and undergrowth but saw no sign of the baby. The older cat by now was with Blackie and her other little ones, but the gray kitten was nowhere to be found. By then we were in a panic. How could the kitten have disappeared?

But disappeared it had, in more ways than one. A couple of days later we found the body of the little one, exactly where we'd been looking all along. Stan and I were deeply saddened, berating ourselves for not having saved the kitten's life. But, fortunately, we can ask seemingly unanswerable questions of the Committee, and this time was no exception. Their response shed further light on how probabilities operate and the free choice that goes into their selection by each consciousness involved.

They said the kitten had not wanted to continue living, and in fact had never planned to live past babyhood. Therefore, its excursion into the weeds was part of a plan, or probability, that the kitten put into place. They said that when Stan and I searched that patch of weeds over and over, the kitten was always there, but in agreement with its desire, we chose a probability where we didn't materialize it. We could have selected a probability where we did indeed see the kitten, and then went on to "save" it; but the kitten would have later found another way to leave physical reality, since it was determined to do so.

I'm not even remotely suggesting we not help our friends in need because they have set their stage of choice. Not at all. For all we know we may become a reason they decide to forgo death, because they find the experience of compassion uplifting or worthwhile; and, of course, our saving them may be part of our own plan to experience compassion. We do what we feel moved to do, for people and animals alike, and if they no longer need or want our help, they will select a probability where we can't interfere with their choices. But meanwhile, they just may be touched by our gestures of love. We surely will be.

Follow the Bouncing Probabilities

How fast do probabilities change? On a moment's notice. In our early days on the Ouija board Stan and I started asking questions about the probability of certain future events coming to fruition, and that type of question, in some form or another, is still one of our most frequently asked.

For instance, one time the question was, "What's the current probability, based on our thoughts, attitudes and beliefs of the moment, that we'll sell the house within sixty days?" The answer: 86 percent. Then we asked again, but now made the time frame thirty days. The answer: 72 percent. As the weeks progressed we kept tabs on the percentage through varied questions, watched it move up and down the probability ladder until it grew quite high, and the house sold shortly thereafter.

Another time I asked the probability of a certain wholesaler picking up *Beyond the Winning Streak* for distribution. It was a relatively low 58 percent, and the next week it was a mere 2 percent. I thought the Committee was joking with the last one, and told them so. They joked back, but didn't change the number. A couple of days later, we got notice that it had been declined.

I started to count on the probabilities they gave us, seeing them as solid bets one way or the other. Big mistake, according to the Committee, because probabilities jump all over the board constantly, based on how we're feeling at the time. To drive the point home, they once gave me a probability of 75 percent on something I wanted badly to see happen. I groaned and said it was far too low. Immediately they swung the pointer to 53 percent. I gasped and yelled, and the percentage dropped to 40 percent.

Finally I started catching on and changed my tune. Now I said how lovely it was that I had a whole 40 percent chance of making it happen—and the pointer went to 55 percent. Then I really laid it on, saying how wonderful it was that I had a marvelous 55 percent opportunity ahead of me—and the pointer went to 81 percent. Sure it was all in fun, but their meaning was very clear. Want to know your percentage of chance of making something happen? Monitor your thoughts and feelings about it. As your emotions swing, so goes your probability. An interesting lesson, is it not?

Here's another intriguing story about probabilities and their volatility. Stan sometimes follows the stock market, and once he asked what the probability was that the market would rise by a certain number. The answer: 25 percent for the leading probability, but there were twenty-seven other strong contenders milling about that suggested other levels of rise and fall. The market closed down thirty points. The Committee said it had been a 5 percenter that came from behind and grew in prominence because the mass beliefs driving the market that day in that particular shared reality (or shared perception of reality) took a collective dive.

Snoward Bound

It was the dead of winter in the Northwest, and I was headed from central Oregon north into Washington. About a hundred miles into my trip I hit the first snowstorm of the season, and it was a beaut. After tolerating inching traffic on fast-icing roads for about forty-five minutes, I decided I'd consciously try to change circumstances and get myself out of that mess. I visualized a sea of probabilities and chose one where I broke free of the traffic and sailed on my way, feeling great happiness at my good fortune.

It wasn't to be. It took me another forty minutes to travel a couple of miles amidst jackknifed trucks and scores of stalled and stuck cars. Because I needed to make a pit stop, I very cautiously pulled off at the next exit, slipping and sliding my way through intersections as the snowflakes deepened into a near blizzard.

About a mile up the road my car refused to grab the ice enough to give me traction, and I found the only direction I could go was in reverse. I backed into a side street, but because of the angle of my car, I was forced to return up the road I'd just traveled. By now I was really worried. Vehicles were all over the place, in ditches, wrecked fender to wrecked fender, frozen in the middle of traffic lanes. It was three o'clock in the afternoon, and dark as midnight.

About the time I realized I could go no further, a motel vacancy sign flashed its welcome, and I skidded into piled snow while looking for its entrance. My car was going nowhere for sure this time, so I grabbed my overnight bag and tramped to the motel's office. As I lifted my eyes into the blowing wind, I caught a glimpse of a restaurant across the street.

After I checked in and got settled in my room, I turned on the news—and quickly came to realize how "lucky" I was. Unbeknownst to me, the traffic I'd hit on the freeway was the start of a one-hundred mile inching line that came to a complete stop shortly after I exited. And there the travelers sat, some for up to seven hours. Not only that, the ones who were fortunate enough to get off the freeway before it slid to a halt flooded the hotels and motels in the area, and available rooms disappeared by four-o'clock that afternoon. My no-star motel room was looking better and better as the televised news progressed, and I didn't even mind the soaked shoes and socks as I plowed through snow banks to the nearby restaurant later that night.

I'd experimented with probability changes with some success in the past, and before I listened to the news unfold I wondered why I hadn't been able to impact the situation. As the hours progressed and more and more horror stories hit the airwaves, I started chuckling to myself. I *had* impacted probabilities. I'd done it! Not to my initial desire, but nonetheless I'd done all right. It's true I didn't "sail on my way," as I'd wanted to, but that was basically the only downside to my predicament. And what a sea of probabilities loaded with disasters I'd navigated, all the way to a warm, dry, non-hungry evening.

Here's food for thought. Why did I need to find a bathroom moments before the freeway literally came to a standstill? Why did my car get into a position where it could only go back the way I'd come, which just so happened to have a motel on my side of the street right when I knew I could go no farther? Why was a room still available, when the motel clerk told me of the growing shortage and the TV later confirmed it? Why was the motel next to a restaurant, when it would have been impossible to walk even a block in search of one? Maybe my visualized feelings of good fortune did indeed help my selection of probabilities. Since I create my own reality, I assume that to be a correct assessment.

Lost Objects Aren't

I was in a hotel room in Minneapolis when I dropped a small inexpensive earring. I hurriedly searched the floor, but due to time pressures I gave up and left for my appointment. Then I forgot about the earring for the rest of my several-day stay. When I returned home I decided to leave its mate in my jewelry holder and see what might happen. The jewelry holder traveled with me on several trips over the next two months, as did the lone earring stuffed into a small compartment. Then one day I opened the compartment and, lo and behold, there sat both earrings.

Stan tells a similar story. A solid gold cuff link that had been lost for over twenty-five years reappeared in his jewelry case next to its mate, which Stan hadn't discarded because of its value. The Committee said we "simply" changed probabilities and rematerialized the objects.

Lost Objects Are

Stan and I were driving to Oregon from a meeting in California one sunny day. Because the meeting was the last item on our business agenda and we headed home immediately thereafter, we stopped at a fast-food place to change into casual clothes. I entered the end stall in the ladies room, an oversized box designed for wheelchair access, and proceeded to undress.

The first thing I did was to remove my earrings and place them on the floor at my feet, then I dropped my clothes on top of the earrings. After I'd re-dressed and started packing my carry-all bag with my discarded clothes, I discovered, to my chagrin, that one of my rather large earrings was missing. I was the only one in the rest room, so I diligently searched not only my stall, but the floors of the other two. I even stripped, shook out my clothes, re-dressed and then grabbed the clothes in the carry-all and waved them around. No earring was to be found.

This is impossible, I thought, that earring couldn't simply have disappeared into thin air—could it? Yes, said the Committee later, it could and did through a change in probabilities. They suggested I "play" with this one, meaning I could alter probabilities and rematerialize it if I tried. I did for a day or two, and then decided it wasn't worth the effort. But I still carry the mate to the lost earring in my purse, and some day I expect to open it and there will be two shiny gold objects side by side.

When It's No Longer an Option

One time I asked the Committee why a certain event did not occur, and they said, "Because you decided it was no longer an option." Is it that simple to change probabilities? Just decide that what seems the most obvious direction is no longer an option? We all establish psychic boundaries around certain areas of our lives that represent the demarcation line between what we will and will not accept. While the line may undulate around the periphery of our off-limits area—meaning sometimes we allow ourselves to step beyond our borders—it eventually becomes firm and obvious.

My sister Pam, for instance, will allow herself to go only so far with a serious illness, and then she calls it quits. One time she was told it had become necessary for her to carry a personal oxygen supply for the rest of her life. Within a week she was completely free of the illness. I asked her what happened, and she replied, "I screamed to myself, in essence, 'No! This is not an option!'" Another time she was told she had a heart condition that would permanently disable her. She screamed and it went away. Both times she hit the electric wire of her off-limits psychic field and ended the problematic situation by not accepting it any longer.

We all do the same thing to varying degrees and drama. Some will push themselves to the brink of bankruptcy, and then cry, in so many words, "This is not an option!" Some will face discrimination only so long, and then cry, "This is not an option!" Yet in other areas of their lives, they're wide open to pain and sadness because they have no established point of retraction.

In my case, moderate to serious ill health is not an option. I may give myself a headache or a drippy nose every once in awhile, but that's about all. I never entertain the idea of illness. I don't fight it off; it just never occurs to me that sickness is a possibility. So strong is my belief in my psychic boundary that when I canceled my health insurance it was without a qualm. It seemed silly, when I thought about it, for me to continue to validate a possibility that no longer existed as an option in my life.

I don't take vitamins. I don't monitor my cholesterol level. I don't check for breast cancer or schedule pap tests. I don't get preventive inoculations or annual health checkups. I assume I'm in menopause, but I'll never take hormones or related medication. I also don't lock my car or home, and I don't carry a rape whistle or own a handgun. I guess you could say I feel I live in a safe universe, and that the only demons that could possibly destroy me from within my body or outside in my environment are my own thoughts, attitudes and beliefs.

Can these psychic boundaries be consciously initiated? Sure. They're built of beliefs, just as all other areas in life are, and therefore can be cultivated by desire. When we change our mind or drop a previously held belief, what happens, in universal terms? We close down one probability, maybe the most prevalent at the moment, and surround our self with others. We halt the forward movement of one probability and sidestep into a field of new possibility. When we stop buying into the idea that a past, present or possible future event is unchangeable, immovable, rock-solid, a given, then we're free to experience other options.

Miraculous Time

Why is it so important whether an event is formed in the present, was formed in the past or will be formed in the future? Because our ability to drastically change our lives depends on our understanding the structure behind the creation of events, and simultaneous time is the obvious key to that understanding. By knowing what we're dealing with, we can use it to great advantage. People talk of miracles as though they are not only outside themselves but larger than life, and yet every moment of their existence they are involved in an intricate dance with the universe that is far more miraculous than a simple parting of the sea.

As Seth tells us over and over, when we come to understand how time functions, we will eventually be able to merge our inner comprehension with our outer perceptions, and then we can form our world on a conscious basis. Can we handle the miracle of a world at peace and value fulfillment for all, if that's what we choose to consciously manifest? That's a tough question. I mean, then we'd have to believe in ourselves instead of an outside source of power, we'd have to believe the world is filled with good instead of evil, we'd have to believe we are the creators of every inch of our lives.

But that presents a problem. Who on earth could we blame if something went wrong?

4

You are in physical existence to learn and understand that your energy, translated into feelings, thoughts and emotions, causes all experience. There are no exceptions.
—*Seth,* The Nature of Personal Reality, *Session 614*

The Ins and Outs
of Reality Creation

Before heading into downtown Portland, Oregon, I perused my to-do list. One of the items was to visit my favorite large department store and start the search for style ideas for some new furniture. I had other reasons to go to that particular store, but since I love studying furniture that one item held my attention. By the time I crossed the city limits I knew my to-do list far exceeded my time allotment. Reluctantly, I crossed off the furniture perusal since it hovered at the bottom of my priorities.

So, in I go to the department store and enter the first available elevator. A couple follow me into it, and we push the buttons for our respective floors. Up we go—and sail right by not only the floor I selected, but also the one pushed by the couple. And at what floor do we finally stop and at which there is no one waiting to board the elevator? The furniture department.

We create our own realities, so sayeth the wisdom of the sages. But the sages forgot to tell us exactly what that means. Sage

Seth says that every event in which we participate, from the minute to the magnificent, was drawn into our lives because we chose
to experience it. Okay, that's the big picture. But it certainly leaves
room for questions when bounced off everyday events and when
we're attempting to understand conscious creation. So, for the rest
of this chapter we'll take a look at creation in general, and our
participation in it. Only a few stories will touch on conscious creation specifically; we'll cover that slice of creation later in the
book.

The implications of what you're about to read are incredible,
at least when compared to mainstream thinking. If understood,
they will lead you much closer to the 180-degree reorientation of
thinking necessary in order to consciously create your desires with
assurance—and finesse. So, enjoy.

Freedom Unlimited

I mentioned in "The 180-Degree Turn" that five people will
view what they believe to be the same table, but actually five tables are projected into time and space. That's because each of us
is in a different space continuum, and in our individual space continuums we create our personal realities. These continuums give
the appearance of one reality created by all, but that's not the
case. We share a *perception* of being in the same place, but technically, we're not.

The reason this becomes so important is because it gives us the
flexibility and freedom to build our realities as we choose to experience them, without limits placed on our experiences from the
exterior. It also gives us the confidence to know that the idea constructions we meet as events are our own, not things foisted upon
us by happenstance. And by knowing we are responsible, we're
free to determine the reasons behind their emergence and to change
what doesn't suit us.

There are basic assumptions that we all telepathically agree
upon, and these don't change because we've chosen en masse to

keep them in place; for example, where countries are located, who the present leaders are, and that there is a structure called the Empire State Building in a city called New York. That part of our shared mental webwork, or shared perception of reality, doesn't alter. But much of the rest is up for grabs.

For instance, if you want a husband and your beliefs and focus are in alignment with that wish, you'll get a husband. It is, after all, your reality. He may not be the one you hand-picked, unless he agrees to participate in your reality as well as his; nonetheless, someone, some consciousness, will step in to fill the role generated by the emanation of your electromagnetic energy units. If you live in poverty and want to experience prosperity, there is not a limitation in your way—if you believe you can do it.

You see, we're the ones who call the shots as to what happens to us, because we create our own realities. The players who enter our lives agree to do so, as we agree to enter theirs, for individual reasons. We can't control the players who decide to pass on our events, but we can control the overall scene. If we believe we're lovable, someone will love us. If we believe we're worthy of success, we'll find it some place, some time. If we believe our health cannot be impacted, we can stand in a room full of chicken pox and walk away unscathed.

Some things can't be altered easily in physicality, such as the regrowth of a lost limb, but otherwise there is great flexibility in what we can create in our individual realities. Seth even goes so far as to say that when we are depressed and it seems the room is closing in on us, it is. It literally becomes smaller and darker, if that's what our mood dictates.

And the converse is true when we're riding high, full of excitement and happiness. The instruments used to measure such concrete dimensional changes would show nothing amiss, by the way, because they would become part of the room's reality and shrink or expand along with it.

The Flexibility of Creation

While we're on the subject of alterations, consider this. You now know that every moment of experience is a fresh one, fueled from Framework 2 in the moment. All items surrounding us right now are brand new, no matter their supposed linear-time life. So, what ages our car, then? Technically, our inner self does in accordance with what we will accept, and that's based on the usual— thoughts, emotions, focus, intent. So, while our car will age because we believe in linear time, the amount and speed of decay is not altogether outside our sphere of influence.

You've seen cars from the 1950s that are in perfect condition. Someone put a lot of thought and focus behind the automobile to make that happen, and, in effect, defied linear time. Sure they painted it, wash it regularly, spend untold hours searching for and installing parts, and lovingly spiffy it up on weekends. That's exactly what we're talking about: focused thought and intent. They love the car and put a lot of thinking into its condition. They get what they focus on: in this case, a beautiful vehicle delivered to them from a friendly universe moment by moment based on the actions they take that express their desire.

But it doesn't always take a lot of physical work. I know a woman who simply believes she won't have any serious automobile problems, that her vehicle will run for years with few repairs needed. She has her car serviced regularly and believes in the guy who does it. She also feels very secure in general, like not much can come into her life from left field that she'd rather not face. Not surprisingly, she is at ease with her car, and it does her the favor of making sure it doesn't upset that ease. In the case of the 1950s vehicle mentioned above, the owner set the car's condition through strong focus and intent; in this woman's case, she set the car's condition through assumption and belief.

Here's another important point about personal creation. Let's say your car's tires are aging. You don't have time right now to get them replaced. Your wife warns you that you're living dangerously, that a flat tire could occur at any moment. Could it? Yes, sooner or later you'll be forced to deal with the reality of the aging tires. But how that reality impacts you is up to the way you structure it. Will you blow a tire on a twenty-mile strip of nothing but highway, or will you drive your car to the tire store over lunch one day, and breeze out an hour later?

Do we find the perfect antique chair, or do we create it in the store we're about to enter? Do we find the perfect blue sweater, or do we create it in the store we're about to enter? If each of us is in our own reality, then there is no reason why we can't create the chair or sweater upon desire. Those who sell the items to us would "remember" that they had been delivered to the stores in the usual ways—but then they are agreeing to the rules of our reality, so why not?

Now about those aging tires. Why can't you simply replace them with a new set, fully installed on the car overnight by elves of the universe while you sleep? If you can walk into a store and find the perfect sweater—and believe you created it—why not the tires? The question is, do you *believe* you could create the tires in such a way? That's probably a stretch, but finding a sweater that you like is completely acceptable within the parameters of what seems possible. So, technically you could create the tires with a wave of the magic wand of thought, but practically speaking, you would have to set aside a whole lot of beliefs in order to make it happen.

Amazing flexibility we're dealing with in our personal realities, isn't it? That flexibility is also why some people miss a scheduled flight that later crashes and why not everyone dies in a plague. It's why some folks experience space aliens and others see the Mother Mary as an interpretation of the same event. And it's why a medicine will work for certain people and why the same medication has no effect whatsoever on others.

The Illusion of Security

As I mentioned previously, I don't lock my car. Stan holds a different set of beliefs, and he feels more secure by taking that precaution. It used to irritate me when I'd leave my car unlocked only to discover in the morning that Stan had slipped out after dinner and secured it. But then one night, without being asked, the Committee brought it up on the board in response to a heated discussion Stan and I had had the previous day on the subject.

They, in essence, told me to drop it, let him be, forget it. They said no beliefs were right or wrong, they were just beliefs. My attitude suggested Stan was exhibiting a metaphysical shortcoming by not believing as strongly as I do in security, but my belief wasn't the better of the two. It was simply different.

Okay, I said, then what are the implications of living with someone with a different belief system? For instance, Stan believes his car can be stolen if he doesn't lock it. I don't. Whose belief takes precedence in this situation? They said, "If you consider the car under each other's control, so to speak, then it won't get stolen because you don't want to participate in that event. Also, Stan has a strong belief that if he locks the car it will be secure, and so it will." They went on to say that Stan's action of locking the car is simply a response to a belief; it doesn't protect the car from theft. Only his beliefs can work such wonders.

The importance of knowing that our realities are created by our beliefs and no one else's is paramount to effective conscious creation. We don't have to worry any longer that someone, some circumstance, some act of fate can keep us from our goal. If we shared a one-reality-fits-all, then that would be the case, but thankfully, the universe was smart enough to build into the structure of our reality the means by which each of us can reach fulfillment, no matter the beliefs or actions of others.

May the Force Be With You

Either we create our realities all the time, or we never do. There is no caveat found in the universal blueprint that says sometimes we're the creators, but other times, well... We're at the mercy of nothing, ever—not someone else's energy, their mind control, their actions. And God doesn't step in and protect us from harm; if we're protected, we've no one to thank but ourselves. Our thoughts, attitudes and beliefs lead us into situations, and they can lead us right back out again.

In the 1930s, my Aunt Marie lived in Atlanta. In those days there was a corner near her home where people desiring a ride downtown would stand and wait for an offer of a ride. It was a neighborly thing to do, and the practice had been going on for years. Aunt Marie didn't give it a second thought when she entered the car of a stranger who asked her if she wanted a lift.

This stranger wasn't playing by the same rules, however. He drove her to a remote vacant building and turned off the ignition. My aunt told me a "cool force" overcame her, and she knew she was going to be fine. She looked him in the eye and told him she trusted him and knew he wouldn't hurt her. Now, she said, take me to my destination in Atlanta, like you agreed to do. He hadn't uttered a word since his first salutation on the neighborhood corner, and he still didn't. When they arrived in Atlanta, he leaned across her, opened the door and silently saluted her. She stepped out and her knees buckled.

Aunt Marie invited the guy into her reality, and he agreed to participate. She then invited him to leave, and he agreed. Could she have been raped outside the darkened building? The answer to that question can only be found in her belief system of the time. I suspect, though, that because she experienced a "cool force," the point of the exercise wasn't to be hurt. Maybe it was to convince herself there really is more to reality than conventional thinking suggests.

Creation on Demand

It had been a busy, hectic eight months since *Beyond the Winning Streak* had rolled off the production line. Stan and I had been immersed in our jobs as vice president and president, respectively, of Seth Network International, which had been born the same month as the book. We had set our priorities and were comfortable with them, but now it was time to transfer some of our focus onto *Winning Streak*.

Being the marketing portion of our team of two, I set my mind's wheels in motion in search of ideas for promotion pieces. Two days later, Stan realized we were running low on book inventory, so he visited the commercial warehouse where *Winning Streak* is stored. For the first time, he was invited to enter the cavernous building and help load the requested cartons onto a dolly.

After lifting a few boxes off the storage pallet, Stan saw a package wrapped in butcher-paper that had been covered by the book cartons. Upon opening it he discovered it held 250 *Winning Streak* covers. The logical explanation was that they had been shipped with the books eight months previously, as I may have decided way back then that they would make good marketing pieces. But neither Stan nor I could remember placing such an order.

A day or two later, before we checked the paperwork on *Winning Streak's* initial print order, we discussed the covers with the Committee. Big surprise, according to them. The covers were created on the pallet the day I decided I wanted promotion pieces. They also said this type of event is not uncommon; in fact, it's normal operating procedure in our reality. And, they said, don't waste your time hunting up old paperwork because it would have been altered in the "past."

A quick refresher course in creation: We are consciousness which constantly creates. With each thought and emotion, we emit electromagnetic energy units that join with others of similar characteristics. The size of the mass that is created from this joining— and its propensity or purpose—suggests the outline of an event that will eventually enter this reality. That event is selected by us from the field of probabilities in Framework 2. Our inner self then forms and inserts the event into physical reality where it enters our life and is placed where appropriate—past, present or future.

Not all remembered past experiences are reshaped by the present. Some hold their contours through the moments as they were originally defined. It all depends on how we're feeling and what we believe in the present that will impact the past.

Anything we wish to experience must first be formed in the mind. We create working models within our thoughts, and then they enter physical reality as actualized events or objects. From depression to excitement, from money to lack thereof, from loneliness to lovingness, it all comes about because of what we think and believe right now. The point of power is in the present, and, if that's the case, thought is the key to that power.

Bettie's Sleight of Mind

If we create our own realities, can there be differences between what you see and what I see? Seth says we telepathically agree on how a scene will look, and then we individually build that scene in our separate space continuums. But, he says, we add our own touches that may not coincide exactly with the creations of others. If our touches become too far removed from the joint consensus, we're called crazy because we're seeing things others don't. But in everyday life, little differences happen all the time and are usually attributed to forgetfulness or mistakes.

Norman Friedman, author of *Bridging Science and Spirit*, an excellent book that compares Seth's material to renowned physicist David Bohm's theories and those of The Perennial Philosophy, has been a frequent guest speaker at Seth Network International conferences. With Bettie Ritchie Kielty, a former British vice consul in Seattle, feeding him questions, Norm explains how the Seth material meets and exceeds the present theories held by quantum physicists. But this story is Bettie's, and it has to do with how we each create our own realities with different interpretations of similar physical matter.

As usual, when it was time to start what unofficially came to be called "The Norm and Bettie Show," Bettie prepared the props for their casual stage chat. When she couldn't find a copy of Norm's book handy, she walked to the conference bookstore at the back of the room, picked up the book she wanted and asked the sales person if she could borrow it for an hour or so. Then Bettie proceeded to walk to the stage and finalize her preparations.

As part of her introduction of Norm, Bettie did her usual: She held up his book so the audience could see it. But this time an odd thing happened when she lifted the book aloft. The audience started laughing. Bettie, not knowing what was so funny, ignored the outburst. The audience, thinking Bettie was British deadpanning, chuckled even more. They thought it was pretty cute that Bettie had pulled a joke on Norm by holding up my book, *Beyond the Winning Streak*, instead of his.

The show finally closed and I approached Bettie, I still laughing at her little joke, and she still not knowing what was so funny. When I realized she was sincere, I told her what happened. No, she insisted, it was Norm's book she held up. No, it was mine, I said. Impossible, she said.

Bettie had read and reread Norm's book, had written a book review on it, had previously used it on stage, had carried it in her luggage and laid it on her bedside table. And yet she "mistook" a white book for a well-loved blue one. Or did she create, in her reality, a blue book from a white book?

Another Bettie story, this one explained by the Committee. In preparation for her second "Norm and Bettie Show," Bettie asked SNI to send her a copy of an audiotape made at the first conference she and Norm had done together so she could study her presentation. Off it went in the mail; back came a phone call to SNI. The tape, it seems, was blank. Off went another, and it was recorded properly, according to Bettie.

But, according to the Committee, so was the first. They said Bettie chose not to materialize the data on the original tape. I asked them that if I listened to it, would I hear the recorded information? No, they said, you would have entered Bettie's reality, and you would agree to her rules. They added that there was one probability where Bettie wouldn't hear the words on the tape, yet I would. "But you see what a dilemma that would cause?"

"Perfect" Mystery

Back to the humorous mystery story of the nuns that I mentioned in "On a Moment's Notice." Okay, so I created the perfect faith part of the book when I needed it. Does that mean the original manuscript of the story now includes the new material? The Committee says indeed it does, at least in my reality. And what does that mean to the people who read the book before I purchased it? It seems anyone with whom I will come in contact who has read or will read the book will agree that perfect faith is an important part of the story. Don't forget whose reality they've entered.

Traffic Woes

So, does "You create your own reality" mean that if we're in the midst of say, a traffic jam, we can uncreate the mass of stalled cars? There are always many probabilities surrounding any event and we have the option of initiating the ones we choose. It's true our beliefs and feelings must be in alignment with our desire, but given that statement, yes, it's a possibility. Once I tried it on a Los Angeles freeway. While Stan drove I visualized intensely and worked at suspending my belief that it would take two hours to go forty miles. The traffic did clear within a reasonable time frame and we passed through the city with relative ease.

But why do I think I impacted that situation? Surely it was coincidence. Well, not if I create my own reality. That means I put myself into the traffic jam and I got myself out. The tough part is suspending a belief held by the masses that Los Angeles is a nightmare for drivers. We telepathically pick up on others' thoughts and accept them as our reality. Not that we have to, it's just easier than the effort it sometimes takes to set a mass belief aside and build one of our own. We acquiesce to others' beliefs all the time. That doesn't mean we can create a reality where Los Angeles is free of automobiles, but it does mean we can create one where we sometimes flow freely and happily through what others experience as hell on earth.

Plastic Events

When we're attempting to work with universal ideas far outside the norm of acceptance, it takes a certain diligence of thought. It's easy to feel powerless to change a situation; after all, that's how we've felt since birth. What takes persistence is the development of the idea that what we see and experience is more plastic than concrete. Successes help to solidify our budding belief, successes that are noted as such and not sloughed off as fate, luck or happenstance.

One day I drove into the back end of stop-and-go traffic on an Oregon interstate, four miles from the next exit. I mentally asked for help out of the mess, not sure I believed anything could really be done at that point except to tough it out. I happened to be in the far left lane, and, on impulse, moved into the right lane—a position I almost never choose.

Shortly thereafter, I noticed a truck about a quarter of a mile in front of me leaving the highway, heading into what looked like a field. As I drew closer, I saw that it was a temporary road used by work crews, and it connected with a secondary road that would lead me to a pleasant country detour. With no concern for the Highway Patrol, I also left the freeway at that point.

Later I got to thinking about the structure of the event, and wondered if I'd created the road in response to my need. No, the Committee said, you didn't. But, according to them, I did bring the temporary exit into my reality by merging my need, the impulse to move to the right so I could see the departing truck and eventually follow it, and the conditions of the exit (meaning it wasn't barricaded to traffic) into my reality.

A Twist to the Real Estate Shortage

A question we asked the Committee one time had to do with the formation of large objects in our reality. Stan and I were driving in the country one day and hit a strip of road where there were no houses for about fifteen miles. We were discussing simultaneous time, and Stan said he assumed that a house could "appear" on that barren strip in the present, just as *Winning Streak*'s book covers had materialized on the warehouse pallet. I wasn't sure, so we asked the Committee that night. Yes, they said, one could. And everyone who drives that road regularly would swear it had been there for fifty years—and it would look it.

Leeway Great and Small

Near our home in southern Washington is a very large white-tailed deer refuge, many miles in diameter. I can't count the times I've walked across the refuge, a singular human surrounded by pastoral scenes of nature and animals. I use my time alone to refocus my thinking and, at times, visualize goals. That refuge is also where I taught myself to alter the weather.

In *Beyond the Winning Streak*, I told of my ability to hold off the rain while out walking my trail, but I drew an incorrect conclusion as to why I was able to alter the weather at that time. I wrote that I assume it is due to two factors. One is because I put emotion behind my desire and then visualize the outcome, and the second is that my thoughts and beliefs, far from the minds and bodies of other humans, are not in conflict with mass beliefs about how the weather will manifest today.

But factor number two is in error. It's my reality and I can hold off the rain if I want to—and if I believe I can. I don't have to be in sight of others to sense their thought patterns. Telepathy is our main mode of communication, if you remember the discussion in "The 180-Degree Turn," and space has nothing to do with the clarity of reception. Since we actually exist in different space continuums anyway, telepathy is our tool for merging our realities into a semblance of similarity. Therefore, I knew what others were assuming about the weather, but I disregarded the input and decided to strike out on my own.

The Committee says it's just as easy for individuals to change weather patterns in New York City as it is in rural Washington. But I don't know, I mean, what is this, our own personal realities or something? When we visit or live in a certain area of the world, we automatically accept its weather parameters. We expect Hawaii to be free of snow and the North Pole to be free of palm trees. These are root assumptions held by our race and we normally don't tamper with them. But within those general parameters, there is great leeway in what we will and will not create as our own.

Stan called me in Washington one day from Oregon. "I heard on the news you had one heck of a snowstorm," he said. "No, it was sunny and relatively warm," I replied. "Must have been a microcosm of special weather over your part of the land," he suggested. I wonder, I thought.

What did the others in our county experience that day? Did some live through a snowstorm, and some don sunglasses? According to the Committee, there's always that possibility. Like everything else in our private reality, they say we create the weather to suit our needs and desires, and everyone with whom we come in contact will verify our version of reality. But, we usually keep our creations somewhat aligned with the masses. Nonetheless, they are our individual versions. If there are five versions of a table when five people enter a room, then there are 3,000 versions of a stadium when 3,000 people attend a high school football game, and there are billions of versions of weather across the planet at any given moment.

It can't be any other way based on the structure of physical reality, otherwise we would be victims, if only to nature. The winter of 1994-1995 was one of the mildest in recent history in the Northwest, or so I heard. I know in my reality it was. I asked the Committee if I'd created my version of the winter in order to help protect and safeguard the health of the many cats and kittens who call our Washington property home. They said it didn't matter what the reason; what was more important was that I realized I'd done it.

True Confessions

While we're at it, I drew another erroneous conclusion in *Winning Streak* that begs clarification. This fact has been mentioned many times already in this book, but here it is again: We cannot be impacted by another's energy unless we allow it to occur. In *Winning Streak* I told the story of Tami, a participant in one of our workshops, who became the guinea pig for an experiment in energy impact.

As a group, we created a negative state of mind in a conference room while Tami, not consciously knowing what was going on, patiently waited in the hall. When she entered the room, she immediately felt uneasy. Within a minute or so, while continuing with the process, she burst into tears, and later said she felt as though she'd been hit in the solar plexus.

We're back to asking, what really happened? Was Tami the victim of our group negativity, as we concluded? Or was she a victim of her own? The exterior events surely seemed to point to our villainy, but when held to the light of universal structure, our conclusion falls apart.

First of all, telepathy is always at play between people, even if they don't realize it. It's how we stay in contact with each other's reality, how we know what's going on in each other's space continuum. Secondly, every event in which we participate is after the fact. We try it on for size, so to speak, in Framework 2 before it enters our reality as a finished product.

So, Tami knew what was happening in the conference room

long before she physically entered it. She gathered data, she decided what she wanted to accomplish based on her beliefs and she chose the probability that matched her desire. We, as the audience, did the same. And together we created "proof" of vulnerability to outside forces.

Are we so fragile that we can be destroyed by a witch doctor's curse or a medical doctor's statement that our disease is terminal? Are we so frail that we can fall under the spell of cults or other people's thoughts? The only question of validity is, who creates whose reality and on what is its construction based?

The Day the Rains Came

One day as I started my walk in the deer refuge, I glanced tiredly at the ominous sky. Oh, no, I thought, I'm going to have to stop the rain today, and I'm just not up to it. Usually when my feet hit the path, all becomes right in my world, no matter what frame of mind followed me to the refuge. But today was different. A chill wind blew at my thin jacket, I'd left my gloves at home, I was weary and cranky. With resignation I erected the glass ceiling in my thoughts, the prop I mentally use to block the rain, but I had to strain to keep it in place. In other words, I couldn't hold the focus on what I wanted to accomplish.

I kept at it, but grew more tired with each step. The sky was dark and the wind continued, but no rain fell. Finally, after about a half-mile, I couldn't go on. For the first time since I taught myself how to block the rain, I said to hell with it and turned around to head back to my car. Not fifteen seconds later, the first water droplets hit. By the time I tugged on the driver's door, I was a soaked mess.

What happened? I dropped my belief that I could accomplish the task I set for myself, and when I did that, I changed probabilities almost instantly. The Committee said later, "See what happens when you give up?" Quite a lesson for us all, is it not?

Whistling Winds

I'm working on another aspect of weather control now, although I don't have my technique perfected, it seems. One day on the deer refuge, the wind whipped itself into a small frenzy, and I decided to see what I could do about halting it. For an hour I visualized the wind abating, using the same technique I apply to holding off the rain. Nothing much happened until I was just minutes from the end of my walk, and then it quieted down.

I felt my experiment was a failure, or at least inconclusive. But the Committee said I did have an impact on the wind, and reminded me of lulls throughout my walk and the wind's abatement at the end. They also suggested that I modify my technique because I didn't quite believe the same process I use for deterring rain would work for wind. And belief is all important.

Will the Real Creator Please Stand?

When Stan and I started the search for our first Seth Network International office, we decided the price range we could afford, the amount of space needed and the area of town we wanted. All of it was based on our beliefs of the moment, and they were based on the reflection of our reality at the moment (i.e., the amount of money flowing into the company, the number of people we thought we might hire over a year's period as a projection of our anticipated growth, etc.). Within three days we found the perfect space and signed the lease.

Now, what really happened in that scenario? Were coincidence and luck at play when we happened to drive by that building and see a For Lease sign? Or did the universe think we were good guys and bless us with the answer to our desire? Do we thank the universe for this bounty of riches or count ourselves lucky? Basically, neither.

Let's give credit where credit is due. We created it through our thoughts. Sure, the universe supported our wishes, and our inner selves even nudged us to drive down that particular street so we might see the For Lease sign (coincidence is part of a solution leading to a desired outcome). But who started the formation of the event, who polished it into a finished product? Thank goodness our inner selves hear our thoughts and help fulfill them; but if we continually assign the fruits of our labors to their side of the ledger, we'll never recognize our incredible power and, therefore, will never consciously use it.

And don't forget that based on our beliefs and attitudes, "the universe" also forms the event that leads to a broken leg. Whom do we thank for that little prize? It reminds me of a conversation I had with a man several years ago. He told me of a woman who was killed when a large piece of construction machinery ran out of control and dragged her to her death. On the same day he rolled his car and came away unscathed. "My guardian angel was with me," he said, with relief and gratitude in his voice. Where was the woman's? Out to lunch?

If the flow of magazine articles and books on the subject is any indication, there seems to be a great deal of interest in the power of prayer right now. And it's true that the results can be spectacular. But what is really going on when we pray? Who actually answers our call?

If Seth is right, when we pray it's our inner self who hears our plea and responds accordingly, not a personified deity. And why aren't all prayers answered? It depends on what people will or will not allow to happen, based on their beliefs and the strength of thought and desire behind the request. If their belief in God's omnipotence and goodwill toward them is strong enough, and they ask for a miracle, they just may pull it off. But watch out if they think they're sinners and God has no use for them.

When we get a grasp on the true nature of our reality, we breathe a sigh of relief that we no longer must rely on God's good wishes to heal our hurts and solve our problems. Surely God must also breathe a sigh of relief; He no longer is called upon to perform miracles that He can't possibly produce because we won't let Him.

After all, it *is* our reality.

Perfect faith is not a belief in God's protection, but a reflection of our belief in the combined power of our inner self and of our outer self, a power that knows no bounds. Perfect faith says we can live our lives however we choose under the guidelines established by simultaneous time and the creative process of thought. It says we have complete ability, based on the structure of our chosen reality, to ask for help and receive it every time we desire it strongly enough, and when we allow.

And why not? We're dealing with a loving energy that has our best interests at heart. It should, seeing that it forms us and sustains us every moment of our life. Our own personal God, you see.

Take Your Choice, Pay the Price

The question that usually comes up following the assimilation of the ideas of simultaneous time and constant creation is, "When an event is over, it's over, right?" I'm sure you've figured out the answer by now, but when it was brought home to me in living color, it did make an unforgettable impact.

I was the guest on a popular Manhattan radio show one day, and the host gave me an audiotape of our on-the-air conversation. Several days later when I returned to Washington, I listened to the tape while out on a walk, and my enthusiasm knew no bounds. Darn good, I thought. I'm getting the hang of these interviews and this one was dynamite.

Weeks went by before Stan heard the recording. We went for a ride on the Washington coast and into the tape player went my prize. But from the beginning I knew something was wrong. Who was this person who couldn't seem to form a concrete idea without hemming and hawing her way through it? What happened to the bright, articulate answers so confidently remembered? I was stunned and embarrassed. Stan was amused.

Had I literally changed the conversation on that tape, and if so, why? The Committee said yes, I had. They said my perception of myself changed over the weeks following the show, and doubts in general had arisen about my abilities. The tape Stan heard was a new rendition of the first, an alteration based on my present thoughts.

Now the question on my mind was, which one was "real?" Their answer: "Whichever you will accept. It is, you see, your reality." So which did I choose? I don't know. I've not had the courage to listen to the tape again. And that is probably the answer.

Deeper Implications for a Sick Kitten

The same little kitten I mentioned in chapter two was ill another day. Stan and I isolated her in the bathroom for a time while we talked to the Committee. Our concern was that she had a sickness that was infectious, and since our house draws island cats like metal to magnet, we worried about the spread of illness. When we asked if Missy Motley had an infection, the Committee replied, "Do you want an infectious cat?" With indignation we said, "Of course not!" And they said, "Well, it's up to you."

"Wait just a minute. We can't control Missy's choice of illness." "No," the Committee responded, "but you can and do choose *your* probabilities. If you want to experience one with an infectious cat, you will. Missy doesn't have to volunteer to be the sick one, but another will step in if she refuses to share that probability with you. You can create your reality, but you can't create Missy's."

It seems we can invite someone to participate in our reality, but whether or not they accept is up to them. Since we reside in our individual space continuums, what happens to me is all my creation, from the literal manifestation of my environment to the probability selections that happen therein. Missy could not be infectious in my space continuum unless I allowed it, and I couldn't force her to play by my script if she chose not to. That, of course, is why my mother can die and move her participation out of my space continuum, and even though I create my own reality, I can't stop her. The agreement between my mother and me to share the probability of her death is decided by us in Framework 2, outside the realm of emotion that would automatically limit our decisions.

Back to Missy. Stan and I chose not to invite a kitten to play the role of an infectious cat, and the proof of that decision was that neither Missy nor another one did so. What still left me with questions, though, was why Stan and I would have considered a probability where a kitten would have been asked to do such a thing. The Committee suggested we look at events simply as experiences, with less emotion driving the questions. It's true that our beliefs, attitudes and desire create our realities, but there is more going on than meets the physical eye.

For instance, assume for a moment I desired to feel needed, and in Framework 2 I studied the options that would fulfill that need. Some possibilities were apparent through my interaction with cats, because they are an integral part of my days. There existed a probability where a cat could become ill and I could nurse it. After exploring the ramifications of the decision, we both gave it a thumbs up. In it then came to physical reality; my need was met, the cat's was met. The cat chose her probability just as surely as I did mine. Why she picked illness is between her and her inner self. But in the spirit of cooperation, we worked out the details and played out the scene.

The Anatomy of Events

Several months ago Stan was searching computer stores and mail order catalogs for a specific $300 fax card for one of our laser printers. They were difficult to find for various reasons and he'd almost decided to accept an alternative solution. Then one day, while exiting a local electronics store after one last futile search of the shelves, he, on impulse, asked a clerk if they sold such a product. The clerk said no, they didn't, but it just so happened that it was being offered as a free gift to all who purchased the same brand of laser printer as ours. He asked Stan if we'd bought our printer at that store, and when Stan said no, the clerk told him to wait a moment while he talked to the manager. The result: Stan walked out of the store with a free fax card.

Another time Stan was interested in a piece of software, and once again for various reasons it was difficult to find. He finally stumbled onto it in a catalog and, with relief, placed an order. Three months later after numerous delays, a company representative called to say they could not deliver the product due to problems with the developer...and proceeded to cancel the order. Not a week later Stan walked into a computer store where he had a passing acquaintance with a clerk. With no knowledge of his desire or search, she said, "I bet you're interested in this software. Just thought I'd let you know that it's on sale, dirt cheap." And Stan finally owned his software.

Is there a universal structure behind such events, or are they the result of coincidence, luck or the gift of a nice guy God/universe? First and foremost, let's not lose track of the fact that we create our own reality. We're not talking about keeping a positive mind-set in the face of our problems, and calling that creating our reality. And we're not talking about toiling long hours on the job, becoming successful and assuming the first was the cause of the second, and calling that creating our reality. We're talking about the whole of our existence, and that means everything, *everything*, that happens to us.

So, let's assume Stan created the situations mentioned above. But how? If you remember, when All That Is created individualized consciousness It also created the infinite probabilities that each consciousness could ever experience. That means that every probable action we can ever take is not only known, it is already a patterned event outside physical time and space. What actualizes an event into physicality? Thought. Beliefs. Intent. Desire. Action.

Stan wanted both the fax card and the software. Each desire created a working model around which events could gather. He thought about what he wanted, pictured it in his mind's eye and took action on his thoughts—meaning he visited the appropriate stores, searched catalogs, placed orders, etc. This activity of thought was responsible for the emanation of electromagnetic energy units from Stan's consciousness, and these EE units drew others to them until they formed a structure that would support the probability of Stan getting what he wanted.

Could he have brought his prizes into physical reality sooner? Sure. If he had expended more intensity of desire over a more focused time frame, maybe he could have moved them in at a quicker pace. If he had assumed he could find what he wanted without delays, possibly he could have owned them sooner. The overriding factor in whether or not his wish was fulfilled was, however, whether it fit in with what he would allow to occur. Remember, Stan was surrounded by all probabilities that possibly could have happened around his desire. He moved from one probability to another as the moments progressed, selecting first this one and then that one to actualize. But there was always a more direct course to his goal, if he had chosen to follow it.

How did Stan just happen to enter the stores that finally responded to his desires? Through intuition and impulse, thanks to his inner self. That's how we find what we want, go where we go. It's the job of our inner self to supply the means to fulfill our wishes, once we have enough strength of belief behind our thoughts to activate EE units into actuality. Stan's process of searching for the goods, thinking about them, and even becoming frustrated at certain turns of events built up the two magnetic fields to the point where they could finally burst forth as the "final" events under the directorship of his inner self.

But there were always active probabilities where he never would have received what he desired. Why not? Not enough desire, intent, focus, belief in himself, in his worthiness, in his ability to find them, in his...on and on, ad infinitum. Thought started the process, thought continued the process, thought slowed it down, thought finalized it—and thought could have stopped the actualization completely. Stan's inner self could have directed his steps to the front door of the computer store, and Stan, using his free will, could have walked away without even realizing what he was missing. We do it all the time.

Breaking the Barriers of Thought

As our ideas of time, space and consciousness expand, we start to break the barriers of thought that have snuggled us into half-sleep, cozied us into half-lives. Simply by seeing ourselves as multidimensional personalities with the power of creation at our fingertips, alive in a magnificent spacious present with ties to great sources of energy outside our reality, frees us to explore far beyond what we've been told is possible—or real. When we can not only come to accept unusual occurrences in our lives, but explore them with enthusiasm for their psychic causes, we bound ahead in our pioneering efforts to understand creation with clarity and intelligence.

Unending questions arise as we forge onward, such as, is New York as safe as Cape Cod to the consciousnesses who believe in a friendly universe? Isn't it ironic to sue for a broken leg caused by a fallen tree on the neighbor's property, when guess who orchestrated the scene? Where does blame fit into the "You create your own reality" picture? And responsibility? Victimization? Aggression? In fact, if no one played victim, would any consciousness come into physical reality to play aggressor? If so, who would the aggressor bully?

Some excellent questions for our race are: How many worlds are there in the field of probabilities and which one do we wish to inhabit? And, maybe most importantly, how do we get to it?

5

In your system of reality you are learning what mental energy is, and how to use it. You do this by constantly transforming your thoughts and emotions into physical form. You are supposed to get a clear picture of your inner development by perceiving the exterior environment. What seems to be a perception, an objective concrete event independent from you, is instead the materialization of your own inner emotions, energy and mental environment.
—Seth, The Seth Material, Chapter 10

Power Hitters of the Universe

"Now, class," the traffic school officer lectures a room full of moving violation criminals, "statistics prove the effectiveness of wearing seat belts. It's insanity not to protect yourself from possible harm, even death, by neglecting to buckle up." Hrump, I think, as I scrunch further down in my chair. What an incredible fallacy! No seat belt is going to keep me or anyone else from bodily injury if we've set the stage for such. It may "protect" us for that moment, if we allow it, but we'll just find another way of hurting ourselves later.

"Who in here wears their seat belt 100 percent of the time?" About three quarters of the class raise their hands. "And how many wear them most of the time?" Pretty much the rest of the room wave their arms in the air. He smiles indulgently at them and scolds lightly, running through the same scenario as before. I think

I'm off the hook, but no way. "Oh," a big smile, like this couldn't be true, but we'll playfully ask anyway, "how many *never* wear their seat belt?" Up goes my lone hand, slowly. A look of incredulity creases his brow. Then he asks me why not.

Here's where my mind comes to a standstill. How do I say to a group of people I've just met that I don't even have health insurance because I simply know I'll never be in an accident or have a serious illness? I mean, come on! This is mainstream America we're talking to, not our favorite metaphysical friend. I mumble something unintelligible, and slink almost off my chair. I have no quick answer for this man, but I'll tell you what. I'm sure glad I hold *my* beliefs, instead of his. Now all I have to do is figure out why I ended up in traffic school in the first place.

Living Our Beliefs

Our lives are crafted from the subjective landscape of our thoughts. Our experience is formed through our expectations, which are reflected in our beliefs. Thoughts, feelings, emotions and attitudes all contribute to the creation of our realities, our lives. They form the blueprint from which events will be chosen and then inserted into physical reality. Our beliefs and intents cause us to pick from an unpredictable group of actions those we want to experience. Until we become aware of what we're thinking and feeling, we can't choose to consciously change circumstances that are not to our liking.

Beliefs are no more and no less than strongly held thoughts, or thoughts held in the conscious mind with emotion, imagination and duration. Strong doesn't mean they are constantly running through the mind, with brow furrowed and eyes squinted. What gives them their power is our *assumption* that they are true, so they cruise through our mind never questioned. But there they go, causing us, consciousness that we are, to emit electromagnetic energy units that gather with others of similar propensity, forming events that make us cringe.

According to Seth, one emotion has more power than it takes to send a rocket to the moon. And, according to Seth, behind every belief is an emotion or feeling. Listen to this list of beliefs, then, and sense their power: Illness is a fact of life. I am a survivor. No one appreciates me. I am a failure. People are so stupid. It's all my parents' fault. It's flu season. You just can't walk city streets after dark. Love never lasts. Money slips through my fingers. Cancer is caused by smoking. Luck and fate rule my life. Misery is part of living. Money is the root of all evil. I am overweight. I am ashamed of my sexuality. I don't know how to love. No one understands me. God punishes.

Forget that you have abundant "proof" that these statements are true. That's the nature of a belief: to cloak itself in justified fact. Of course it does—what we believe becomes real. The question is, which came first, the chicken or the egg? Jane Roberts says, "Our senses present us with a lovely package of the world. We hardly ever realize that it's a do-it-yourself kit; that at other levels we put the pieces together, assemble the ingredients then present the entire box to our conscious selves, pretending it's a surprise and something entirely apart from us or our creativity."[1]

The starting point for the creative cycle is thought. Thought causes us to feel a certain way, and that feeling starts the emanation of electromagnetic energy units. The EEs join together and form various size masses with different intensities, and those masses eventually become material objects or events in our lives. Since a belief is a snugly held thought, the intensity behind the EE units emanated by the consciousness which holds the belief is extraordinarily strong.

But what happens, cosmically speaking, after a belief or thought is expressed in the mind of consciousness? Seth says the mind is a great organizer, and since a belief reflects an assumption about reality, the mind prepares itself to support the assumption by organizing reality to fit the belief's definition. And how does the mind carry out this not-so-little feat? By forming events that agree with the belief; by gathering data that supports the belief; by selecting probabilities that reflect the belief. No matter what it is we believe, the power of the mind will sculpt our reality into a dramatization of the belief.

The Mind at Work

One time I was a guest on a television show that seemed to have gone all wrong. From the host's first question I felt she and I were at cross purposes, that her choice of direction wasn't what we'd agreed upon. Because of the need to move quickly through discussion, I felt we weren't developing the ideas I wanted to express fully enough for the audience to grasp their significance. I assumed the host agreed with my assessment because her body language seemed to support my on-the-fly analysis. When I left the studio I was drained and distracted.

Stan, who had been in the audience, thought it had gone smoothly, but on the other hand he pointed out hitches that I also had noticed. After dinner that night with friends, one of them pulled me aside to discuss the show, which he had watched from his home. He enumerated the exact "problems" I'd seen with it.

That night in our hotel room, I awoke from an uneasy sleep with the event on my mind. But the source of my unease wasn't the show, per se; it was because I knew that the show's supposed outcome was being reinforced by me with each negative thought I put behind it. Since an event is never technically over in this universe of ours because we select our past, present and future moment-by-moment in the now, I started wondering what it would take to alter the TV show as I remembered experiencing it. I didn't just want to accept that I'd do better next time, I wanted to make that event literally become better than its first iteration.

The most obvious issues that needed to be addressed were my feelings about the outcome and the beliefs about myself that led me into the situation in the first place. I thought a lot about what the Committee says about it being easy to change beliefs by changing our emotions; that simply by saying—and meaning—"whatever happened is no longer an option" can work wonders, and that there's nothing to stop us from switching from one belief/emotion to another in the blink of an eye. So I settled my restless body down and gave the process a try.

I started clearing my mind by releasing my concerns and drawing myself into the present moment. Then I smiled and told myself that, hey, I did just fine. I let that roll around my thoughts for awhile, and then I started thinking about the next day and the day after that. I saw myself telling others how great the TV show had gone, and I relaxed with the idea that I could make my choice right now as to what I wanted to experience, not only in the future, but in my past. I said to myself, "The point of power is right now. Choose your thoughts and feelings wisely." Then, after maybe ten minutes of unabashed smiles and little chuckles, I turned onto my side and went back to sleep.

A day later, Stan and I viewed a video of the show for the first time. I felt a twinge of concern just before it started, but then I smiled to myself and said, "What the heck. Relax and enjoy." It took no more than one minute of air time to know it was all okay. None of my original concerns were justified by what I saw on-screen. I heard a pleasant repartee between me and the host and reasonable answers to most of her questions. We seemed at ease with each other, and she was knowledgeable on my subject, which was the Seth material.

I can't tell you how elated I felt as the show ended. I absolutely knew I'd impacted the outcome of that event, that I'd re-selected probabilities by changing my thoughts and beliefs through conscious choice. Not that the show was a stunning success, but it was good. I felt free and excited, ready to try consciously altering an event again—well, maybe not immediately.

An interesting thing happened the next night. I received a fax from my friend who had seen the same original problems with the show as I had. He still saw them. His fax listed several issues he felt could have been handled differently, and the overall tone of his missive was one of disappointment in the outcome. As I read it I thought, I can't relate to what he's saying; surely we viewed two different events. Later I asked the Committee why, if I'd changed the past, did my friend still hold a reaction to the original version. They said he was reflecting a residue of my previous beliefs back into my reality.

So, what happened throughout this ongoing event—and what happens to all of us all the time—was that my mind, the organizer that it is, went to work immediately during and after the TV show to help me justify my ill ease. My friend volunteered to play the role of critic in order to validate my beliefs that the show had been awkward. When I altered my beliefs, the video validated my new ones that the show had gone well and I had done okay. Then my friend popped back into the picture to validate lingering, but weakened, beliefs about the whole thing.

The important issue to grasp is that the mind will do whatever it takes to create the picture of reality as we believe it to be. Therefore, all beliefs will be justified in terms of physical data, meaning they will take on shape and form in our lives, whether they are to our detriment or support. A person who feels she is poor will lose, misuse or badly invest any amount of money, whether she works hard for it or is given it. A person who has hypnotized herself into a state of loneliness will always be lonely, whether surrounded by friends or holed up at home. We always seek out those situations and feelings that conform to our beliefs, and avoid those that don't.

Mind Magic

The Screen Actors Guild (SAG) union card is difficult to come by at times for aspiring film actors, or so my daughter believed. With a bachelor of arts degree in theater, some non-union film and television acting, and a lot of stage work in regional and university theaters under her belt, Cathleen dreamed of the day she'd become a bona fide card-carrying SAG union member so she could steer her career in her direction of choice.

She had been working with a casting agency which had sent her on many auditions over several months time. When she had listed with the agency, Cathleen mentioned that she was not a SAG member. One day, one of the staff members told my daughter she'd been cast in a union film job without an audition, and Cathleen reiterated her non-union status. The woman's reaction was read by my daughter as one of mistrust, as though Cathleen hadn't been honest with her from the beginning about the lack of a SAG card. The film job went away.

After that, the phone calls from the agency stopped. Cathleen felt it was due to the misunderstanding. Since the casting agency was the largest in her metropolitan area and placed the most talent, she was very upset and concerned about the situation. Then one day about six weeks later, the agency called her again and sent her on a film audition for a union part. Bemused by the situation because she thought the agency surely remembered her non-union status, Cathleen went to the audition and won the role. When the agency called to discuss the part, Cathleen once more mentioned that she was non-SAG. The agent was surprised. No union card, huh? Well, not to worry. And the agency arranged to get her the coveted card. My daughter was now a SAG union member.

What happened in this scenario? Cathleen badly wanted to join the Screen Actors Guild, and she also felt that without the SAG card she was not "professional" enough in people's eyes, not to be taken seriously, a mere amateur. Her mind then set about proving to her just how the doors would close and how she would be treated without the sought-after union card in her possession. She selected a probability where the casting agency seemed miffed by the misunderstanding and, therefore, dropped her from the work list.

But what happened between the time the phone calls stopped

and the SAG card entered Cathleen's reality? At first she wallowed in worry and self-doubt. She told her friends of the situation, and they mirrored her concerns back to her. They hashed it over and tried to figure out how to right the wrong. Finally, Cathleen had had enough. She decided it was time to change. Having a metaphysical background helped her see how she was compounding the problem through her negative focus. She knew she had to change her attitude and beliefs if she wanted to move on.

The first thing Cathleen did was to release her pent-up emotions. She simply decided to let them go. She stopped buying into the belief that her acting future had ended in that metropolitan area and decided that, with or without the casting agency behind her, she'd make it. She started telling her friends that everything was going to work out fine. The ongoing discussion among Cathleen's actor friends was the major difficulty of obtaining a SAG membership. She, remembering how reality is created and believing it, told them not to worry; they would all get their cards no matter what.

In essence, Cathleen modified her beliefs about her abilities, about the potential of the future, about what she wanted out of life and what it would take to get it. She reset her thinking and started believing in herself again. She did a little visualization for another job, which she didn't get, but the focus on a positive future set the stage for greater possibilities. That change in her thinking then caused the selection of an event from the field of probabilities that brought her a dream come true.

The mind works magic. It's the ultimate organizer, the consummate builder of realities. Our thoughts design the blueprint and then the mind goes about its business of matching events to expectations. We get what we believe we'll see in our world.

Snake People

Several years ago, Stan flipped on the television late one night searching for the news. Since I never watch TV and seem to have an ingrained method of blocking its sight and sound from my consciousness, I paid no attention whatsoever to what he was doing. But a documentary that was on the air quickly caught my attention because its whole premise reflected the power of beliefs.

Have you ever heard of snake worshipers? That may not define their activity accurately, but it seems there are fringe Christian churches or cults that use poisonous snakes in their services. Stan and I watched in fascination for about fifteen minutes while very deadly snakes of different varieties were held, kissed, stroked and wrapped around necks, all to prove that these people were God's chosen few and therefore protected from harm. Some, but not all, of the small congregation joined in this rite after working themselves into a state of frenzy through music, dancing and incantations.

Then, after playing with the snakes for some time with no apparent bites, several men drank what was said to be pure strychnine—again, simply to prove how protected they were by God. And indeed they were protected. At the end of the program, the news team which filmed the scene announced that they had had the liquid in the labeled strychnine bottles tested, and it was true and pure poison. And the venom from these deadly snakes— snakes which usually bite these people with regularity, although that's not what happened this evening—was found to be just as true and pure upon testing.

According to the people who participate in these snake sessions, only the deeply believing ones survive—but those folks go on for years getting bitten and drinking poison without apparent side effects. We're back to asking, what is really going on here? Is it God who's protecting them? Or is it their *belief* that God is protecting them that makes them immune to danger? There is a great underlying lesson to be learned from these snake people, and a greater one about the ultimate power and organizational abilities of the mind.

Feeling Our Way Through Life

The fabric of our life is composed of certain continuous strands of thoughts and beliefs homogenized into a feeling pattern. That feeling pattern is our emotional attitude toward ourselves and life in general, and it governs the large areas of our experience. Our feeling pattern becomes the active backdrop for our daily life's events, and our individual beliefs and emotions become the stars that shine against that backdrop. But the backdrop determines the overall picture of where we're headed in life, and so it must be considered as a major player in the creation of our reality.

For instance, some people may have strong, supportive feelings about their ability to be successful in life, because they believe they make their own luck or can manipulate circumstances to their liking. They feel confident that little can be done to stop their forward movement because they can handle anything that comes their way. They see themselves as emotionally strong and generally fit. Overall, they have a healthy attitude toward themselves and others, and an optimistic overview of life.

That attitude becomes the stage for their life events. An illness hits, seemingly from out of the blue, but it won't keep these people derailed for long because they have this wonderful undercurrent of feeling pattern that all will work to their advantage in the end. They may get fired one fine day and hit the depths of depression—but not for long. Soon they will rise to the occasion by allowing their ingrained feeling pattern to kick in and move them beyond the pain.

So, from a metaphysical viewpoint we know these people created their illnesses due to their beliefs and they got fired due to their beliefs. We also know they pulled themselves out of both pits due to their stronger beliefs in their overall abilities. Both kinds of beliefs must be understood and recognized when we start consciously creating our experience.

I know a man who missed that point, and it was his undoing. He worked with conscious creation for years, but he never saw the bigger picture of his life. He analyzed the beliefs that caused him to become ill, or broke, or hurt. But he never realized that his overall feeling pattern was incredibly pessimistic. In fact, he never would have applied those words to himself if backed into a corner. He saw himself as rational, logical, coping with what life dealt him to the best of his ability.

But under it all, he looked for the worst to happen. If a minor unsettling event occurred, he dwelled on it, projecting its effects into the future via his feeling pattern about life in general, and so compounded the problem—and verified the beliefs behind his feeling pattern. This went on year after year, wearing him down until he decided not to go on any longer. Finally he simply gave up and died. It just wasn't worth the effort to continue when he could not seem to break the depressing cycle of haphazard constructions, or so I deduced.

Fortunately, not all beliefs are rock-solid. They flow with the feeling of the moment; they change when we're up, or change when we're down. Say we're really excited about something, imbued with a zest for life, then our belief in personal vulnerability may be put on the back burner as we sail through events that at other times would have had us biting our nails to the quick. This feeling of zest can become part of our feeling pattern, if we cultivate it. Then it automatically sets the mood for our days—and by default, creates our life along its defined lines. It becomes part of our philosophy toward life and, by its nature, exerts a tremendous force in shaping our future.

Does it not behoove us then to take a closer look at what runs through our minds all day long, or what long-term attitudes and feelings we've held without ever questioning their value? You bet. And that brings up an important point, one with which many psychologists don't agree, thanks mostly to Freud. Beliefs are always found in the *conscious* mind. We don't have to fear a subconscious attack from beyond rational thought, or years of psychoanalysis to dredge them up to the surface. According to Seth, beliefs ride the waves of conscious thought constantly.

Our problem usually is that because our beliefs have become assumptions to us, they are never questioned and, therefore, never recognized as beliefs. It's similar to posting a note to yourself on your bathroom mirror, perhaps something inspirational that you want to remember frequently. How many days go by before you fail to see the note, so cleverly has your mind relegated it to background mode? It's the same with your beliefs.

Just don't lose track of the fact that the conscious mind is a mighty tool, there for the using. It may need taming and training, but that's about it. The conscious mind is well equipped to see its own beliefs, reflect upon them and study their results as they develop in our physical world. So using this tool, the mind, as it was meant to be used, would automatically help us recognize both our beliefs and their effects. Then we could evaluate their validity and whether or not we wish to continue in the direction they automatically set for us.

Belief Spotting

If we really seek change in our life, we must become aware of our beliefs. It takes study and thought, and maybe persistence, but it's possible to learn to not only see our own beliefs, but those of others as well. What we sometimes find as we start building our awareness of beliefs is that the search seems overwhelming. One belief leads to another to another to another, and then we wonder if we've really found the "right" ones, those we wish so desperately to recognize and change.

But, take heart. Seth says, "As you examine the contents of your conscious mind, it may seem to you that you hold so many different beliefs at different times that you cannot correlate them. They will, however, form into clear patterns. You will find a grouping of core beliefs about which others gather....They <u>are</u> consciously available."[2]

Since everything we experience is a reflection of our thoughts and beliefs, they're behind which emotions we feel, what actions we take, the condition of our bodies, the possessions we own, our thoughts of the future, the guilts we harbor. Our lives unfold based on our beliefs about ourselves, our upbringing, our past, the condition of the world, our prejudices, our views of religion, health, illness, safety, vulnerability, love, money. They can be seen in living color in the kind of friends we choose, our fears, our home and work environments, our reactions, our selection of career, the associations we join, our political positions. What we believe, we experience.

Let's take a look at some limiting beliefs that are held by many in today's world, and as you read them, try to gauge your reaction to each.

- Sickness cannot be escaped.
- Viruses attack randomly.
- I am helpless to heal myself.
- Luck and fate control my life.
- I am a victim of circumstances.
- No pain, no gain.
- It's a dog-eat-dog world.
- I was so little and they hurt me so.
- I must work hard for the money I earn.
- Money is the root of all evil.
- To want money is not spiritual.
- Suffering is to be expected in life.
- I am powerless to significantly change my life.
- Evil is a fact of life.
- I have nothing to offer the world.
- I am vulnerable to crime and accidents.
- No one understands me.
- I'm not attractive enough to find a mate.
- No one loves me.
- Love comes and goes.

Now, let's take a look at some positive, supportive beliefs, and, once again, as you read them try to gauge your reaction.

- I am a good money manager.
- It's okay to be rich.
- I deserve lots of money.
- Life is so much fun.
- The universe is with meaning and purpose.
- The world is a safe place to live.
- I believe in myself completely.
- I am competent and successful.
- I love who I am.
- I am at ease with my body.
- I can handle whatever comes my way.
- I am a decision maker.
- I am worthy of love.
- I take responsibility for my whole life.
- I am filled with energy and enthusiasm.
- I control my health through my beliefs.
- There is no illness I cannot heal.
- I will die peacefully and comfortably.

There our beliefs sit, hardly noticed by us because they are an integral part of our daily life, accepted as fact. Take the way we handle commonly accepted minor illnesses, for example. We assume we'll get a cold this winter because we always do. Yes, flu's a definite possibility, especially since we've been exposed to it by the neighbors. With spring right around the corner, better stock up on allergy medication. No telling how long this back pain will last, but I'll bet it's not going to go away quickly.

We program ourselves into situations through our thoughts and beliefs. We really must become aware of what we're thinking in order to change repetitive life experiences that make us uncomfortable. In *Beyond the Winning Streak* I discuss several processes

I've used over the years to find beliefs, notably one I call the "Belief Root Diagram." It can help you recognize beliefs by following your emotions back to their source—which is always a belief. I also discuss using muscle testing as a means of identifying beliefs. Muscle testing is a simple and effective method of communicating with the mind by using the muscles of the body to verify what you believe about a given area of your life. It's quick and easy, yet the answers you receive are quite dramatic at times, and sometimes loaded with insight.

Just for the fun of it, during a cozy evening alone query yourself for answers to these questions on abundance and then ask why you answered as you did. You'll find yourself looking your beliefs right smack in the eye.

- Are you anxious about money? Do you feel that no matter how much you make, it's never enough?
- Does money come easily to you?
- Is your self-worth tied to money?
- Is it always "in the future" when you will "have money?"
- Do you envy rich people? Do you feel contempt for them? Do you think they look down on you?
- Do you hesitate to enter ultra-exclusive boutiques? How do you feel the clerks will treat you?
- Do you think you won't have enough money until you are older...degreed...married...promoted...or whatever?
- When you see someone driving an expensive car, what do you *feel* about them? About the car?
- Can you create your own wealth? Do you need to rely on a mate?
- How do you feel about lending money?
- What is your definition of a greedy person?
- Do you feel that outside financial forces (such as taxes or fate) control you?

Now try it with these questions on self-worth, or better said, what you really think of yourself—and don't forget to ask yourself why you answer as you do.

- When you're in a group, do you sometimes feel unsure of yourself? Worried that your opinions won't be accepted, listened to or taken seriously?
- Do you have difficulty making decisions?
- Do you tend to let people think you agree with them when you don't?
- Do you ever make yourself do something you would rather not?
- Do you freeze when called on to talk in front of a group?
- Are family and friends always judging you?
- Was there ever a time when:
  Someone made you do something against
      your better judgment? Why did you do it?
  You felt prevented from doing something you
      wanted to do? Why didn't you do it?
  Someone took advantage of you?
  You felt like a martyr?
  You felt misunderstood?
- Do you have fun most of the time, or are you burdened with problems?
- Do people look down on you?

Once more, give it a try with these questions about your job or career. Can you identify what's holding you back?

- What characteristics do you dislike or resent in your boss?
- Pick a co-worker you don't get along with: What are that person's traits?

- Does your boss trust you...scare you...control you...not understand you...not recognize your potential?
- Do you resent having to work?
- Do you dislike or resent the work you do for a living?
- Do you feel locked into the job/career you now hold?
- Is your present position beneath you?
- Is your present position too far beyond the scope of your abilities?

Listed in *Beyond the Winning Streak* are many pages of beliefs, both positive and limiting, broken down into these categories: money; spiritual/religious/life; self-worth; job/career; relationships; health. Either study these lists, find other ones or make up your own, but do something about familiarizing yourself with beliefs in general and your personal ones in particular. There are few gifts in life you can offer yourself that will bring greater rewards than to recognize instantly when a thought has become a belief.

Creation by Default

Our thought processes automatically take us in the direction of unconscious acceptance. When we *assume* an event can happen because of this or that, we literally seed the future with its likelihood. It is vital, therefore, that we become aware of thoughts that we are projecting in time.

For instance, you're low on money. The busiest season for your retail store is not for three months. Because you can't see into the future, worry arises. You start to plan for eventual hardship, you scope out the option of borrowing funds, you think about what you could cut out, ways of scaling back. You remember your kid's next dental appointment and wonder whether or not it should be canceled. You eventually draw some conclusions and put a plan of action into effect, all the time hoping like the dickens the outcome will be favorable.

Now let's look at the situation from the standpoint of universal structure. You are consciousness residing in a physical reality where the one "law" is that thoughts create. You're here to learn just how amazingly consistent that law is, in fact. Being consciousness, you are imbued with the ability to create whatever it is you *think about.* Your thoughts trigger emotions which activate those dear little EE units into action. They prepare themselves to become an event or material object, based on your train of thought and the intensity behind it. They start coalescing into a structure, and as you build the picture of the future in your mind, they move to create it for you.

And what you've done is given them the definite impression that you've accepted a certain general outcome and made plans accordingly. Never have you assumed the money could show up in the next day or week or month. Never have you assumed a joyous—or at least satisfying—event could occur that would change the picture entirely. Never have you twirled thoughts into emotion into EE units that cast the future with exciting possibility. So, never will you experience such an event.

We must stop thinking that planning for the worst is logical and responsible. What it is, often, is self-defeating. It's time to forget or at least minimize our belief in what we've been taught since childhood about how to solve problems by analyzing today's "facts" and drawing rational conclusions from them. The acceptance of this line of thinking automatically sets a process into place that can lead to personal grief. By its nature it usually assumes the worst, and we don't even question the assumption behind the thought. It becomes a bridge into our future, because it structures our thinking along definite lines.

Not that we only fall into that trap when faced with important decisions. No siree. We do it throughout our day. Yeah, the day after tomorrow is really going to be a drag, with all the work that's piled up. I don't think I can afford a vacation this year because my taxes are going to be sky high. I'm sure there are going to be problems when I tell my kid he can't use the family car this weekend. I only have one month until my manuscript is due, and I don't think I can make it. Good Lord, I ate a yogurt with an expiration date of a month ago! Now I'll probably get diarrhea.

See how rational we are? No Pollyannas in this room. No siree. We look the bare facts in the face and call a spade a spade. Not for us the unfounded, illogical thought that says everything is going to be just fine. No siree. No fools allowed in this room.

It isn't that we should drop all backup plans and fallback positions. But for heaven's sake, we've got to start sensing other probabilities and assuming that physical reality is based on a very consistent rule that works in our favor once we understand its basis.

Decision-Making at Its Finest

Here's further thought on the search for Seth Network International's office space that I mentioned in chapter four. Stan and I determined what our needs would be for the coming year and projected that scenario into Framework 2—and out came office space that exactly met our desires.

Since events enter our lives based on what we expect to see, they are actually fiction created by us, for us, as experience. They simply verify our mind-set. Stan and I got exactly what we projected into Framework 2, but was the size and cost of the office space based on beliefs that reflected a limited amount of growth? If we had seen or sensed a more successful upcoming year, what would we have created for office space? Did we automatically stifle greater success by not allowing its possibility into our thinking, at least at that point in time?

What most of us seek in order to make pressing decisions is usually more information. That normally means we scour the exterior world for facts and figures and wrap them into our thinking. Eventually, we make our decisions based on most of the information available to us. However, the "facts" gathered in the outer world are simply ones we expected to see, hoped to see, or chose to see. And from those facts, we set a future course through assumption.

What's wrong with this picture? Maybe nothing, maybe a lot. Since each of us puts our own picture in place, and the picture is a snapshot of our private interior world, we can assume it is awash in the coloration of our beliefs. If our beliefs are strong and success-oriented, the facts found in the exterior world will head us in a direction that leads to success. If our beliefs are grounded in fear or limitation, the facts we gather to us will reflect that mind-set.

So, how do we make decisions solely on exterior-world facts? Hopefully, we don't. Hopefully, we gather further data from the interior world before making final decisions. That information, of course, comes from our inner selves through the inner senses and contains data from a broader picture than our conscious minds usually pick up.

Because our inner selves not only see today's beliefs but the probable paths our future thoughts and beliefs might take, they can make educated guesses as to what we'll choose to experience. Those guesses, fed to us in various ways, such as through intuition and insight, will allow us to alter our decisions to ones more in line with a probable future that holds greater potential.

But the educated guesses made by our inner selves go by the wayside if we change our attitudes, thoughts and focus. If we lose faith in what we hope to accomplish after we've set our goals, their projections can slide off the horizon. On the other hand, if we build faith in our ability to consciously create our future, we may achieve astounding success and meet a future event far beyond what seemed probable a short while before.

This is where perfect faith comes in. If we know we're constantly supported, that there is a structure to the universe that is in place specifically to lead us into our own personal value fulfillment, then our thoughts and beliefs can more likely stay loose, less fearful, more filled with anticipation. Perfect faith becomes a powerful belief held in the moment—and you know what happens in Framework 2 based on our beliefs of the moment.

It's not only our faith we need to build, though. It's that 180-degree reorientation of thought that's needed: the reorientation that tells us that what we see in physical reality is after the fact, that it was formed in Framework 2 first, based on our thoughts and beliefs; the reorientation of thought that tells us that what we *think* while viewing or participating in that after-the-fact event is what will select our next probability. With that knowledge and perfect faith under our belts, we can start to break the belief in cause and effect and free ourselves to consciously utilize the tremendous power of the moment.

As Goes the Mind, So Goes the Body

There I sat in the airport lounge, kicking myself for having created a sore eye. For several days I'd been at a conference where different issues had arisen that I'd allowed to irritate me and, bingo, I created the symbolism in the form of a scratchy, watery eye. It was now mid-afternoon and hours since I'd awakened with the problem. As the plane entered its assigned airspace, I dropped the back of my seat and decided enough was enough.

What I needed to do, I knew, was to drop my irritation at the events that had occurred and the people involved. Obviously, how I had chosen to view the conference was my reality, and I could change it by changing my beliefs and feelings. So I cleared my mind, released my judgments, saw it as the play it was—selected, directed and acted by me in alignment with my beliefs—and then fell asleep. I awoke twenty minutes later to a clear, pain-free eye.

Seth says, "The inner self keeps the physical body alive even as it formed it. The miraculous constant translation of spirit into flesh is carried on with inexhaustible energy by these inner portions of being, but in all cases the inner self looks to the conscious mind for its assessment of the body's condition and reality, and forms the image in line with the conscious mind's beliefs."[3]

Maybe there is more important information to know about the body, but it's difficult to imagine what it might be. That Seth quote is the bottom line, so to speak. Whatever—whatever—the body experiences, the mind has made it happen. If you know a way to bypass your beliefs when you create your reality, let me know. As far as I can figure, they control every aspect of physical existence, and our bodies are no exceptions. Some day when I'm out of this world, I'm going to find Errol Flynn and ask him why he died with the body of a seventy-five year old when he was only fifty.[4] I'm just nosy enough to want to know what beliefs aged him ahead of his time.

In *The Nature of Personal Reality*, Seth makes the comment that, "Natural hypnosis and conscious beliefs give their proper instructions to the <u>un</u>conscious, which then dutifully affects the body mechanism so that it responds in a manner harmonious with the beliefs. So you <u>condition</u> your body to react in certain fashions....Daily behavior and chemical functioning smoothly follow according to the belief."[5]

Linus Pauling, twice the recipient of the Nobel Prize, died of cancer at age ninety-three. To many people his name is synonymous with vitamin C. He not only championed the belief that vitamin C builds healthy bodies and prevents certain diseases and illnesses, he lived his talk by taking 18,000 milligrams per day. He advocated megadoses to treat cancer and prevent common colds. Pauling believed his ingestion of vitamin C delayed the onset of his cancer for twenty years.[6]

Did it? Possibly so, but his strong belief in the need to *protect* the body from disease also may have set the stage for the cancer. "To protect from" means there must be something threatening lurking in the wings. It's an acknowledgment of a belief in vulnerability to something outside the self. If the world's population chose to drop the mass belief in cancer, would it disappear? In a second. Can we individually drop our belief in the killing power of cancer? Most certainly.

That's what happens when a person is cured of the disease. Believe it or not, there is logic behind the "miracle." Somehow, some way, the ill person radically changed her beliefs, intent, attitude and focus, and that altered what her inner self could insert into her life. No longer did her inner self have to keep re-creating the old condition; it could now give her a non-cancerous body. That's what happens with faith healing, too. The person suspends her day-to-day beliefs in her lack of power and assigns God the responsibility for curing her. Luckily she believes in God so the belief works in her favor; that she never comes to understand her role in the drama is not important to the outcome.

But her body isn't just changed in the present. Seth says, "A sudden or intense belief in health can indeed 'reverse' a disease, but in a very practical way <u>it is a reversal in terms of time</u>. New memories are inserted in place of the old ones, as far as cells are concerned under such conditions. This kind of therapy happens quite frequently on a spontaneous basis when people rid themselves of diseases they do not even know they possess."[7] Ah, the flexibility of time and space.

Instead of becoming more at ease with our beliefs, we seem to be spiraling out of control in many areas of life on earth. The baby boomers in some ways have come to represent the current thinking of the masses, and because of their great number, their beliefs become highlighted in the media. According to a new study, baby boomers are much more likely to get cancer than their grandparents were at the same age. And the study's researchers insist the increase cannot be fully explained by "smoking, better diagnosis or an aging population."[8] They don't know what's causing it, but speculation says one culprit may be "as yet unrecognized environmental hazards." How about mass beliefs in a world out of control, life that has lost its sense of purpose, and a lack of understanding of what causes disease in the first place?

Some people are fighting back in their own ways, maybe spurred on by their inner selves to be participants in an exercise that shows the world the power of the mind. For instance, one of the most comprehensive studies on the placebo effect was recently announced.[9] The placebo effect is defined in the study as "a natural healing ability triggered by belief in a treatment, doctor or institution." Actually, that's a great definition of how we heal all of our ailments, whether given drugs by a Western doctor or chicken blood mixed with tree bark by a witch doctor. But, back to the study.

It's thought placebos work in about 35 percent of patients. Asthmatics, given an inhaler filled with water, experience the expansion of their airways if told the inhaler contains a potent new drug. A study of 2,504 back surgeries showed that even when no problem was found—and the patients were simply stitched back up—43 percent had relief of pain anyway. Say the researchers, "The placebo effect influences patient outcomes after any medical treatment, including surgery, that the clinician and patient believe is effective." Yes, indeed.

Seth: "...You can become healthy if you are ill, slim if you are overweight, gain weight if you prefer, or alter your physical image in profound fashion through the use of your ideas and beliefs. They form the blueprint by which you make your body..."[10]

Role-Playing Through Reality

The Committee once said, "All the marbles are yours. It's up to you as to how you play them." Does that little gem of wisdom mean we choose everything, I mean *everything*, that happens to us? Yes, according to Seth. He says, "You create your own reality. There are no exceptions." No exceptions means no exceptions. We cannot believe we're victims to accidents, another's infection or second-hand smoke if we believe there are no exceptions. It does not mean that we won't allow outside sources to impact us at times, but it most definitely means it will be our beliefs that move us in that direction, our beliefs that will determine if and when the outside source will harm us—and if so, to what extent—and our beliefs that will deepen or lighten the situation.

Usually about now someone will bring up the subject of babies and children, because it's very difficult for us to accept that little ones have already formed beliefs that lead them into what we view as serious trouble. When we see the world as immersed in linear time, with a definite beginning and ending to our lives, then the philosophy of "You create your own reality through your thoughts, attitudes and beliefs" seems to make no sense when applied to the young.

When a mother recently killed her two little boys by drowning them, I searched my mind for an explanation of how that exterior event was created. No answer seemed "logical," until I remembered that Seth says we couldn't function in physical reality without an enormous data bank of information and experience already built into our psyches at birth, and that includes the beliefs we have chosen to integrate into our beginning years of life on earth. The body starts afresh, but the mind never does.

So, why would the little boys have chosen to die such a horrible death? Maybe the question should be reworded to, "Why does consciousness choose to experience what we in physical reality view as horrible events?" The answer might be, "Ask them next time you meet, and listen as they tell you what they got out of it." The first question is loaded with our limited-reality slant on life and death; the second neutralizes the emotion and removes the question from our usual sphere of understanding; and the answer tells us there were choices made and directions selected.

When we enter this reality we come prepared to experience many things of our choosing, and we set the groundwork in advance. Form and event always follow belief, so before birth we mold into our consciousness certain attitudes and ideas that will start us on our overall path. We're not talking karma here; we're talking the wish to experience certain feelings and events for our own personal reasons—yet with the built-in flexibility to change our minds at any point in time. In the little boys' case, the Committee said they had probabilities at play right up to the "end," where they could have opted not to continue with the script. But decisions were made to go ahead and act out the scene.

Where does the mother fit into the overall picture? She had the same number of options as her boys, of course, and she chose a path and made it happen through her beliefs, focus and intent. That we disagree heartily with her choice is not the issue at the moment; when we remove the emotion from the event, a structure can be seen that allowed it to be played out according to the final arrangement between mother and sons. Our lesson, as consciousness trying to grasp the implications of probabilities, idea constructions and their effects on ourselves and others, is to judge our reaction to the event and challenge our own thoughts and beliefs that led us into a probability where an event of that nature could occur.

We live in a very cooperative reality. We play many roles for each other, but as actors, we only select those that fit our backgrounds. If someone asked me to play murderer to their victim, I'd unconsciously refuse: I don't have the qualifications for such a role (i.e., beliefs that lead to feelings of powerlessness, deep anger, or whatever else it takes). But, because this is such a cooperative reality, some consciousness with a more acceptable resume will volunteer. It does make one wonder just what our world would be like if none of us had the beliefs that qualified for either murderer or victim, does it not?

Cosmic Butterflies

If we're so smart, why ain't we rich...or healthy...or loved...or happy...or peaceful...or...? When only 33 percent of Americans feel safe alone at night on public transportation, there's massive work to be done with beliefs in our culture.[11] We can't look to others to solve our problems through legislation, money, social and health programs, or education. Nothing, that's nothing, will work that comes at us from the outside. Policies and programs are put in place by people as reflections of their beliefs and the beliefs of their constituents. In an odd way, the conditions these people seek to reform are reinforced, because they so strongly believe in the truth of the conditions.

The only solution to global, national and social problems is to change individual belief systems. Finding our beliefs is only a piece of the overall puzzle, albeit a very important one; changing them, as we'll discuss in chapter 7, is really the key. So, until we return to beliefs, I leave you with this Seth quote, one meant to tell us it's all okay, we can do it, we can figure it out, we can find our way out of problems and into happiness: "For, if you trust what you are, you can never go wrong, in whatever terms you use. You can fly through belief systems as a butterfly flies through back-yards."[12]

6

Consciousness is, among other things, a spontaneous exercise in creativity. You are learning now, in a three-dimensional context, the ways in which your emotional and psychic existence can create varieties of physical form. You manipulate within the psychic environment, and these manipulations are then automatically impressed upon the physical mold.
—Seth, *Seth Speaks*, Session 515

Minding the Magic of Life

Our lives are intricately woven masterpieces, crafted by us, for us. Our creativity, our gift of the gods, is the thread that weaves the moments into days, and the days into years. It's the underlying basis for our experiences, the source of our magic. In the last chapter we focused on beliefs, but they are but one facet of our creative natures. Although it's our creativity that allows us to build beliefs and more intricate systems of beliefs, from it also springs other aspects of our being.

Emotion, intent, imagination, focus, assumption and belief magically homogenize into what we call our life. They flow together, inseparable, one substance from which all else emerges. The creativity that hones our days is formed not only by what we believe, but by what we feel and what we assume, by what we imagine and what we focus on, and by our overall intent and purpose.

Beliefs form the cornerstone of life and underlie our days, but it's impossible to bring major change into our reality without addressing the whole picture and without using the magic of our creativity to do so. To consciously create means to become the conscious implementer of that creativity—and then get out of the way so the magic can happen.

Conjuring Up a Future Event

One afternoon I entered the Moline, Illinois, airport with ticket in hand that would take me to New York City for an interview on a late-night radio talk show. But I quickly learned that, due to a blizzard in Denver, a major airline hub, and terrible weather in other parts of the country, the skies were going crazy. No planes were arriving in Moline on time, and none were leaving even remotely close to their scheduled departures, if at all. The airport was frantic with passengers trying to re-book to other flights— myself included, since mine had been canceled.

That New York radio talk show was a plum, and I decided that I absolutely didn't want to miss it. So, while standing in what seemed an unending line awaiting my turn to talk to a harried airline representative about getting me into the air as soon as possible, I started visualizing. Seeing that showtime was in less than five hours, I imagined walking into my hotel, baggage in hand, smiling at the clerk, casually registering and sauntering to my room to relax a moment and freshen up before the show.

The first thing I was told when I finally reached the airline ticket counter was to forget it, that it was an impossibility to get to New York until morning. But while the ticket agent was running through the computer's litany of flights one more time, I kept up the visualization. Finally she found a seat that had just opened on the last plane to Chicago, and since Chicago is closer to New York than Moline, I took it. I raced for the gate and reached the plane just in the nick of time.

Almost all the way to Chicago, I continued visualizing. I knew

I had to drop the anxiety, or at least dampen it, so I made a concerted effort to relax by not thinking about time and by allowing myself to have a little faith that I could pull this off. I decided not to look at my watch again until I landed in New York.

Once we arrived in Chicago, it turned out to be an instant replay of Moline: no New York flights available until morning; horrendous lines to be maneuvered; and finally a seat that opened up at the last minute on the last plane into the New York area, which was actually headed for Newark. I grabbed my new ticket and ran, thinking that my visualizations hadn't included so much exercise and stress. The pilot had bad news, though, as he taxied onto the runway. We were to be grounded for maybe an hour due to a backup in traffic. There it goes, I thought, my last chance. I can't possibly get to Newark in enough time to get a taxi to the radio station. But, what the heck, I'll keep visualizing and ignoring time.

Don't ask me what happened, but time somehow adjusted itself for me. I eventually got to Newark and got a cab after learning that my luggage was still in Moline and would not arrive until morning. I looked at my watch for the first time since leaving Moline. There was actually time to go to the hotel first and at least check in.

But my story doesn't end there. As I was returning to the hotel from the radio station, in walks a guy carrying my luggage. Big surprise. It had arrived on my flight with me, but for whatever reason had not been placed onto the carousel. How it managed to make the last-minute plane to Chicago and the last-minute plane to Newark can only be answered by the universe. Ditto for how I got to that radio station with five minutes to spare.

Magic Happens

Magic, that's all it was. That's what allowed me to use my creativity and select an event of choice. Magic is what forms our world and our bodies, it's what charms our life into being. Underneath everything we experience is magic as real as...well, as real as All That Is. To use the magic in fun ways, to play with it, doesn't take much. When we set an idea in our mind and hold on for dear life, magic happens and the idea becomes real. When we joyfully throw emotion behind a desire, magic happens and the desire comes to fruition. When we play in the charmed circle of our mind, magic happens because All That Is set it up that way...magically.

When Stan and I checked into the airport on another trip for a red-eye flight from Portland to Chicago, we were told all but two seats were booked. Since we wanted to spread out my computer and his computer books between three seats, I decided to see what I could do with visualization. Once we were seated on the half-filled plane with an as-yet empty seat between us, I propped my lowered head in hands and "saw" us sprawled in comfort for the next four hours.

As I finished my visualization, I glanced up and into the eyes of a fellow passenger a row ahead of me across the aisle. His face reflected compassion, and if I understood his summation of the situation, he empathized with my need for prayer before flying into the unknown. When no one came to occupy the vacant seat, he may even have been sincerely pleased for me—a worried traveler with at least extra space for comfort.

What were the magical pieces at play in the Moline-to-New York and Portland-to-Chicago events? What ingredients had to be creatively held within my mind in order to manifest the desired results? Certainly assumption and expectation had to play a part, and so did imagination and emotion. This extraordinary mixture, this magical recipe, is exactly what each of us automatically uses to get whatever it is we want—and sometimes don't want. We simply don't recognize the magic with which we play as anything special.

But it is incredibly special, because we touch the creativity of All That Is when we believe in it, and just as important, we touch the magic in ourselves through faith in the universal structure that supports us. Seth says, "Faith in a creative, fulfilling, desired end—sustained faith—literally draws from Framework 2 all of the necessary ingredients, all of the elements however staggering in number, all the details, and then inserts into Framework 1 the impulses, dreams, chance meetings, motivations, or whatever is necessary so that the desired end then falls into place as a completed pattern."[1] We are magical creatures wallowing in creativity—and that creativity starts in the mind.

Mind Images

Nothing will enter our reality unless and until we can see it in our mind's eye or sense it. We must be able to conceive of what we want through image or sensation, and then we can bring it into reality as a working model. But if we can't get a basic internal picture formed, we'll never have it. We must see or sense ourselves pulling into the gas station or walking across the carpet before either event can materialize. It may be so fast a focus that our conscious mind almost misses it, but still it must happen. Everything we create starts with a thought translated into an image or sensation. From falling down the stairs to winning the lottery, we simply must be able to think it's possible and then see or feel it happen.

I had to know my arrival in New York was a possibility and then see myself there in order to experience it. If instead I'd pictured myself searching for a hotel room in Moline, or sleeping on a bench at O'Hare, I could have walked into those events. Idea conceptualization and visualization form the natural method of identifying which probabilities we will encounter, and many times it's done without obvious awareness.

Usually, the stumbling block to the biggies in life is that we can't see ourselves in the position of ownership. If we live in a ghetto and have never experienced riches, the gulf between the two lifestyles may seem vast indeed, so vast we can't grab hold and believe wealth is a possibility. Movies splash glamour across the wide screen and magazines often describe scenes of upscale living, so it's not that we're blind to such alternatives. But can we see *ourselves* in the picture? One time a guy told me he really wanted to own a red Corvette. His desire was strong, and finally his dream car showed up—across the street in his neighbor's driveway. When we discussed it, he said he still didn't feel comfortable seeing himself in the driver's seat. He couldn't visualize it or believe that he could own such a fine automobile. And so he couldn't.

What we focus on takes on form and shape, at first in our mind and then in the exterior world, because, as Seth says, "Form is the result of concentrated energy, the pattern for it caused by vividly directed emotional or psychic idea images. The intensity is all important."[2] When we concentrate on an idea or desire, the mass of electromagnetic energy units generated by that concentration is great, so great that a portion of our own consciousness is actually imparted to the form.

Intensity is the core that draws the EE units into an eventual mass, and the stronger the intensity or emotion, the sooner the mass enters this reality. It matters not whether the intensity is formed around a fearful event or a happy one, a consciously chosen event or one we entertain through unconscious focus, the result is the same. The old saw that goes, "Be careful what you ask for; you just might get it," is true, if the idea is held with intensity and emotion. Seth says, "Emotions, instead of propelling a physical rocket, for example, send thoughts from this interior reality through the barrier between nonphysical and physical into the "objective" world—no small feat, and one that is constantly repeated."[3]

To go where we want to go in life means we have to know where we want to go. If we never identify goals by bringing them into our mind as concepts, the foundation to a future of choice is never laid. We'll still get a future based on our goals, but those goals will be formed by default through lack of conscious intent rather than directed focus. If the goal is to join the unemployment line every Tuesday for six months to collect compensation because we assume there is no other path open to us, so be it. If it's to find a job that reflects our internal feeling of worth, so be it. We will get what we can conceive of, and there will be no judgment placed on our selections by the creative powers-that-be. So, where do we *see* ourselves in the future? Wherever it is, that's where we'll be.

Maybe the thing to do is decide in advance what you want out of life so you're not taken by surprise. Some people hate goal-setting. I'm not one of them. To me, seeing my objectives on paper somehow strengthens them in my mind. I've changed my personal goal process over the years, but basically, I select my choices for three categories: short term, long term and life. The short term list includes what I want to accomplish from the immediate moment to within a year; long term encompasses the time frame beyond one year; and life goals are personal issues I want to address all my life for my own growth. Every six months or so I re-address my goals, fine-tuning as necessary, but at least once a week, maybe more, I study my list and think about what I'm attempting to accomplish.

I don't consider this a dull and boring exercise. According to Seth, "Your intent, images, desires and determination form a psychic force that is projected out ahead of you, so to speak. You send the reality of yourself from your present into what you think of as the future."[4] If that's the case, then goals start the process of forming our future because they reflect the first conceptual ideas of what probabilities we wish to entertain through conscious intent.

Images Made Manifest

Seth says, "To act in an independent manner, you must begin to initiate action that you want to occur physically. This is done by combining belief, emotion and imagination, and forming them into a mental picture of the desired result. Of course, the wanted result is not yet physical or you would not need to create it, so it does no good to say your physical experience seems to contradict what you are trying to do."[5]

When I set my goal for wealth back in my days at Apple Computer, it wasn't even remotely close to my reality. I had to conceive of it and then *do* something, or take action, to make it happen. In fact, I did a lot. Since it's a story in itself and is told in *Beyond the Winning Streak*, I'll not repeat it here. But I will talk about the mighty tool of imagination, because it's what molds our conception into a working model.

The true power that we, as consciousness in a physical reality, hold is latent within our imaginations. Imagination, which speculates upon the unexperienced or unmaterialized, brings life to desire. When backed by great expectation, imagination can activate almost any reality within the range of probabilities. Visualization, or directed imagination, is simply strong, clear thought applied to our desired goal. We see the outcome we want to experience, we feel it, we live it. We build up the intensity of our desire through focus and we assume our goal is happening. We expect it. We have faith in its outcome. *We imagine it.*

When Arnold Palmer was twelve, he set his future direction through imagery. Whenever he played alone, he staged a mock tournament. He pictured the whole scene, from the voices of the crowd to the physical setting. He heard the announcer call him champion, and he felt the emotion of the win. Jack Nicklaus states in his book *Golf My Way* that his good shots are 10 percent swing, 40 percent setup and stance, and 50 percent mental picture.

Whatever we desire may be manifested more quickly by using focused thought during an altered state of consciousness. Seth says an altered state can shorten the connective time between our creation being formed in Framework 2 and its result in the physical world. Our desire might be stated as a goal we want to pursue, a material object we'd like to own, a statement of belief we wish to solidify, a general request to hear our inner self more clearly, a more targeted desire to receive guidance for, or a solution to, a specific problem, or whatever other reason we choose.

Sometimes it helps to set the stage, so to speak, for working in an altered state of consciousness. Select a quiet room where external noise can be kept to a minimum. Perhaps light a stick of incense. Play soft unobtrusive background music. Dim the lights, and maybe light a candle. Choose a comfortable position and relax your body. Close your eyes and quiet your thoughts. You'll want to make your imaging as vivid as possible, but don't worry if it seems a stretch to do so; words work equally as well as images for some people.

So, what do you visualize? Do you focus on a definite goal or the bigger picture? There are few parameters that need be set around visualization, but here's food for thought. After studying probabilities, you know you can't force a person to become the love of your life if he or she chooses not to participate in that role. But you also know that if you wish to be loved, some consciousness will answer your call. That suggests you keep your visualizations more open, less focused on an individual and more on the feeling you wish to experience.

Personally, I think that's how I'd approach a situation like that one. But I'd also hold the desired person's face in my mind throughout the day, keeping him in my thoughts so that if he's agreeable to entering my space continuum as my lover, I'd be developing that probability. But if no interest is shown on his part, I'd have to remember that my goal is to be loved, so in my visualizations I'd let love permeate the scene without picturing a prechosen individual. Instead I'd have a vague or undefined figure play the role I scripted.

After that's said, however, here's the other side of the coin. At times I've been very detailed and selective in what I want to see occur, and it has manifested. So maybe the best advice is no advice. Develop your own scenarios and see what happens. Learn when to cut your losses, and change your visualization when your wish is not manifesting. Play with the universe in fun. Ask for guidance from your inner self, and stay open to possible shifts in direction. What the heck, we're talking about your life. Come at it from this way and that until you hit upon a formula that works for you.

Visualization efforts are never wasted. The EE units you generate will be applied to some event in your field of probabilities, even if they don't immediately coalesce into the exact scenario you want to experience. If an event occurs that isn't directly related to your visualization but still reflects part of your desire, acknowledge it as a direct result of your work. Give yourself credit for your creativity. Change sometimes comes in small packages for awhile and then hits big time, but it's always predicated on your efforts.

How much does visualization impact the outcome of an event? Once my actress daughter wanted a specific acting role. She applied visualization and eventually was told the part was hers. According to the Committee, there was a 12 percent probability Cathleen would get the job when she first heard of it. As her desire grew, even before she started visualizing, the probability rose to 67 percent. Then visualization took it to 100 percent, and the director called to tell Cathleen the good news. In my case with the Moline-to-New York event, the Committee later said I'd had but a 10 percent probability of making it to the radio station that fateful night. Visualization came to my rescue.

At times I've done my homework and nothing has come to pass. Whatever it was I was visualizing never occurred. Why? My beliefs may have blocked the desired outcome, I may not have strongly desired it, I may not have held my focus in place long enough. At times the reason is apparent to me, other times it isn't. But I know one thing for sure. If I didn't get what I wanted, the stumbling block was in my mind, and my mind alone.

Magic in a Nutshell

The magic of life has been condensed into a relatively few

paragraphs in this chapter. But it really does get down to some basics that are easily stated and rather apparent when bounced off the structure of our reality. In the next two chapters we'll learn how to apply the ideas discussed here to personal situations, but for now, just get a sense of how the imagination, combined with emotion and focus, makes things happen. As a quick review, here are some helpful hints on how to consciously form your desires into actuality.

- Conceptualize your wish
- Set a goal for it
- Imagine it
- Focus on it with emotion, desire and intensity
- Assume it's possible

We've Only Just Begun

What an incredible reality we live in, what a marvelous playground to experience. How very fortunate we are to be surrounded by magic that fills our every desire, supports our slightest whim. We are truly blessed children of the universe, gifted with incredible power and the brains to use it. We all have the inherent ability and capability to walk into our goals, objectives, desires and wishes with aplomb, striking the pose of success when and where we choose. That we need to finesse our creation technique seems obvious at times, but we're well on our way now, headed into our personal field of dreams.

Look out world, here we come!

7

Your conscious mind is meant to access and evaluate <u>physical</u> reality, and to help you chart your course in the corporeal universe of which you are presently part. Other portions of your being ...rely upon you to do this. All energy at the inner self's disposal is then concentrated to bring about the results asked for by the conscious mind.
      —*Seth,* **The Nature of Personal Reality,** *Session 627*

Consciously Creating Change

My daughter phoned one day in a state of agitation. At the time, she was in college and her furniture from previous apartments was stored at her father's warehouse. She'd just learned that he had sold her washer and dryer without permission because he needed the space. It may have been an inappropriate action on his part, but what Cathleen and I discussed was why she, as consciousness creating her life based on her beliefs and attitudes, would have allowed it to occur. My ex-husband could not have entered her reality, or space continuum, to participate in that event unless there was a telepathic acceptance by Cathleen. It never could have happened without my daughter's consent via her mental signals. It was Cathleen's selection of thoughts that led to the incident. A different set of beliefs—perhaps about herself and life in general—

would not have drawn in such an experience from the field of probabilities.

Cathleen's task became to figure out why she reflected into her reality the feelings of helplessness and lack of control. As long as she continued to thrust her anger onto her dad, she would never identify the real creator of the situation, and so would possibly never become aware of the mind-set that walked her down that path. And she also would be projecting her anger and confusion into the formation of electromagnetic energy units, which would then draw more events to her of a stressful nature.

Part of the solution to understanding an uncomfortable event such as Cathleen experienced is to figure out what within us gave the event the power to enter our life. What role did beliefs play in the situation? Simultaneous time? Probabilities? Emotion? Assumption? Then, once we've thought it through—perhaps more to understand the structure of events in general than the one we dissect in particular—we start to get a sense of what's behind our personal creations. We become aware of patterns of thought, or core beliefs, or repetitive emotions that link one uneasy event to another, even though the events seem to have nothing in common.

Once we've identified limiting repetitive themes or decide we want more out of life, the next question that arises is, "How do we change what we don't like about what we're creating?" The answer to the question is not a simple one-liner. It takes moving from theory and philosophy into practical application and finding methods to put our knowledge of universal structure to work for us in the most fundamental of ways. If we've been given the gift of the gods—the gift of creativity—then it's time we started consciously using it.

The Practical Universe

Knowledge by itself will not bring great change into our personal or global life; only application of that knowledge can turn a sow's ear into a silk purse—or haphazard constructions into abundance and health. So, we'll build the power platform of success securely under our feet by using our knowledge, thoughts, emotions, desire and focus to propel us into our dreams. And that means applying ourselves to the process of change.

Because we live in a practical universe, practical steps can be taken that will direct us to where we want to go. In a reality constructed of ideas and fueled by activity, it makes sense that the way into what we want and the way out of what we don't want are built of the same basic ingredients: thought and action. It's just a matter of implementing ideas that will move us in our direction of conscious choice.

There is no one path that fits all, no cookbook approach that leads humankind to nirvana, no ultimate set of directions that prépares the way for riches bountiful. We are all so different, being consciousness with unique propensities, that no magic list is possible. So we will suggest some thoughts, techniques and exercises that you may want to explore if you choose, or discard if you will. All of them are grounded in Seth's concepts of the structure of our physical reality, and three of those key points are once more summarized below.

- *Consciousness Creates Form*
  We are consciousness which has chosen to enter physical reality and play with its building blocks for our own reasons. With every thought and emotion, we emit electromagnetic energy units that join others of like propensity and eventually manifest physical objects or events based on our intensity of focus.

- *The Point of Power Is in the Present*
  There is no linear time per se; there is only simultaneous time camouflaging itself as linear for our learning purposes. Since time is simultaneous and we reside in a spacious present; since we're surrounded by every possible probability

that can occur to us; and since the past and future are built in the moment based on our probability selections—which are based on our thoughts; then all the power of life resides in the now.

- *We Are Connected to a Great Source of Power*
  Every moment of our life is governed by our inner self, that portion of our greater self that keeps us alive and creating in physical reality. Through its direction and assistance, we manifest our physical world based on our thoughts, emotions and beliefs. One way we can learn to consciously use this power of creation is by listening for our inner self's advice and following it when desired.

Using these concepts as our knowledge base, and weaving them into our reality through acceptance and practice, leads to the 180-degree reorientation of thinking that is necessary to do what we want, to become whom we choose. They place our feet on the smoothest possible road to conscious creation. So, what all of the techniques and suggestions you'll learn in this book, when homogenized into a whole, will help you do is:

- Focus on the now
- Learn to identify beliefs
- Learn to change limiting beliefs
- Drop your belief in the past
- Imagine the future
- Listen to your inner self
- Assume you can make *anything* happen

Please remember when you're working with these exercises that you are doing something extremely powerful. You'll not just be mouthing superficial words or fantasizing fluff. Nothing that we think and feel—*nothing*—goes unnoticed by our inner self. If we act as though we're ecstatic over a future event we're projecting in visualization, our inner self will accept our sincerity and do what it can to make the event happen. If we say and believe we have incredible power at our fingertips, our inner self will start the ball rolling to help us prove the point. *All thoughts and emotions create.* It matters not whether they are generated "naturally" throughout the day, or put into place consciously. So don't downplay the power of inner work. If you do, so will your inner self.

According to Seth, these types of exercises should be repeated for up to ten days for maximum effectiveness—or until you know in your heart you've created the outcome to your satisfaction. Which could, of course, be immediately.

Affirming the Point of Power

The underlying theme that runs through all of the suggestions and techniques in the next two chapters deals with the importance of simultaneous time. The immediate moment, or the now, is where our strength lies, so it must be utilized to its fullest for the best conscious creation results. Easy enough said, but when we've been indoctrinated into the theory of linear time very thoroughly, it sometimes takes desire and persistence to break its hold on our belief system. But where better to apply our focus? After all, if our point of power is in the present, that suggests it's to our advantage to develop our ability to reside there with ease.

Picture this: Surrounding you is an infinite field of probabilities, representing all possible variations of events you could ever experience. See these probabilities as bright tiny sparks of silver against a background of black velvet. Now see many larger gold stars randomly spread throughout the field. These gold stars represent the probabilities that are most likely to be actualized in your life, based on this moment's thoughts, attitudes and beliefs.

Now, pretend you change your thoughts from, say, fear to excitement about an upcoming event. Look what happens to the field of probabilities. Some silver sparks become gold stars, and some gold stars become silver sparks! Now change your attitude about a past event and see what happens. Same thing. When we change our thoughts in the present moment, we change the most likely events that will lead to and from the present.

If we remember that the point of power is right now, that *now* is when we select the events we will encounter in life, then we can start to utilize our incredible ability to build our life as we choose. Seth offers us a great affirmation to help us become successful conscious creators, one that can literally change our life if we believe it: I create my reality, and the present is my point of power.

Repeat this phrase over and over to yourself, post it on your mirror, on the dashboard of your car. Think it before you fall asleep, awake to its litany. Fashion it into a jingle and sing-song yourself to work in your car. One way we enter new beliefs into our mind is through self-hypnosis. That's exactly the tool you're using with this exercise.

Breaking the Bonds of Fear

When we believe in cause and effect, we also tend to believe that if we are fearful of something, we have a right to be. After all, look what happened to me last week, or last month or twenty years ago. That's when it started, that feeling of fear, and I've had cause many times since to meet it again. It's been with me awhile now; it's no stranger in my life.

But, according to the structure that makes our physical reality happen, fear can't be based on yesterday's cause, and here's why. Fear is an emotion that follows a belief, and emotions are generated in the now with the surfacing of a belief; and then an event will follow that reinforces our fear because it's selected from the field of probabilities by our emotion of fear. In other words, fear has to be generated by a belief about something *before* another fear-filled event can occur, whether the event is a physical assault or a simple twinge of anxiety while reading news of violence. Fear is based on an active belief.

It may sound like a bout of semantics, but it's an important point. Fear is generated in the moment by a belief held in the moment, and between the two of them they tell the mind to organize our past to reflect their influence. So the mind sets to work and chooses probabilities that are placed into our "past" that verify the fear. Fear is not intimately tied to our past, building as the years progress. It can't be. It's tied to our present.

That we *feel* that fear has been with us forever on a given issue is because we think we remember concrete past events. But the remembrance of the past is selected in the now. Our life fans out forward and backward from the present. What we think and feel right now pulls in probabilities, some of which we will call past and some we designate as future. All creation happens now based on the workings of our mind now.

Feelings aren't stand-alone items; they must be flared into action by thought. Fear is not held over from our last foray into the depths of anxiety, imprinted on our minds from the past, or unbreakable until we take our last physical breath. Since emotion follows thought, to break the cycle of fear means to break the course of our thoughts. Seth says, "Your emotions trigger your memories, and they organize your associations. Your emotions are generated through your beliefs. They attach themselves so that certain beliefs and emotions seem almost synonymous."[1]

So what we need to do is set aside whatever it is that's causing the fear. We have to break the cycle of thought that leads us into the emotion of fear, because fear sidetracks us, derails us. In response to fear, we literally select events that block us from our goals. Healing, mentally and physically, takes place when we clear our minds in the present and give it room to accept new instructions.

There are two ways to stop fear: 1) find and change the beliefs causing it, and 2) break its hold in the now. We'll cover how to find and change beliefs later in this chapter, but now on to a technique for stopping fear dead in its tracks this very moment.

Anxiety is a form of negative visualization, exceedingly effective. Break the visualization, break the anxiety...and break the probability of a future worrisome event. We can't stop thinking, but we can control the focus of our attention. Since two thoughts can't be held in the mind at the same time, we can give precedence to the one of choice. So, let's test our ability to halt a little fear that most people have felt at one time or another. Let these words become real to you right now, feel the anxiety they generate: I don't have enough money to pay my bills. Now say in your mind, "Wait, there are no successive moments, so there is no past!" Let the tension leave your body instantly. Say, "This is my reality, and I can construct it any way I choose right now." Then insert a positive response that offsets the fearful one.

If this were a real-life situation, you'd now hold on to this feeling of calmness and clarity, and think to yourself something like, "Okay, I've created a limiting situation in the present that looks solid, but I know there are other probabilities I can choose. Since there is no linear time, I can restructure this situation by allowing other choices to enter my life." If you can stay in the now, believe everything will work out all right, have perfect faith in your power as consciousness in physical form to choose your direction consciously, you walk the path of new solutions to your perceived problem.

Sometimes it's no more difficult to break the cycle of fear than to acknowledge that fear is something that can be consciously set aside by choice. Break the fear, and at times it actually breaks the belief at the same time, without the need to go any further with processes or programs. That is the ultimate, isn't it? To move through life with ease and a sense of complete ability to live each moment as we choose, without the need for artificial constructs such as techniques? We can do it, you know. It may take "time," but we can reach that state of being.

Living in the Now

Here's another technique I use when I feel myself slip into the old way of thinking—that is, when I'm concerned about something or fear what might happen in the future. I say to myself my favorite one-liner once again, "There are no successive moments." For me, that statement has such emotional impact that it immediately breaks my concentration on the issue at hand.

While I'm saying it I drop all thoughts from my mind and look at my surroundings. I see everything in clear focus, studying colors and textures and shapes. I quickly release all tension from my body. I smile. I feel the freedom this knowledge of simultaneous time brings to me. And then I think, "My life is mine to build *exactly* as I want to experience it. I am surrounded by other scenarios. This one is no longer an option."

Defining Your Now

I carry around a paper with me at all times, tucked into a pocket or purse, but always easy to access when I feel the need. I especially make sure it accompanies me on my long walks through nature settings, because I tend to do much of my inner work then. It's titled "Selecting Future Probabilities: How I Need to Think and Feel in My Now," and here's what it says on it.

> 1. Sense my inner self with me, moment by moment, listening to my thoughts, advising me. *Feel* it here with me.
> 2. Remember that moments don't flow successively. They are piecemealed together based on what I think right now, and form the future in that mold. That means projecting hopeless, fearful thoughts into the future only arranges the now to create that future's possibilities.
> 3. Feel perfect faith in myself and the universe. What perfect faith held in this moment does is re-

lease my thinking from limiting future projections. It keeps me in the now.

4. Sense my goals as completed events around me now. This makes them as real as my supposed present. They have the same validity and strength—and reality.

What reading these four points does for me is to remind me of the structure of the universe and how it's there to support my efforts to change. I read my paper if fear surfaces, but I also read it just for the joy of the message. If I'm in my car, or in a light altered state, sitting quietly watching the river or walking on the deer reserve, I'll take many minutes to absorb each statement, thinking about what it means to me as consciousness in physical form. The process almost always does a magical job of drawing me out of my focus on a problem and puts everything into a very different perspective.

White Board Assistance

When learning to stay in the now, one of the most difficult things for many to do is to break the cycle of unhelpful thoughts and feelings that insist on running through their minds, thoughts and feelings indicative of the belief in linear time and cause and effect (i.e., I screwed up that project once before, so why do I think it will be different this time?). One night, in response to utter frustration over not being able to consciously set my mind in the now and hold its course, I had a dream. I saw my mind as a white, blank slate ready to accept completely new scripts as I wrote them in the present.

From that dream I developed a technique I call the "White Board." Sometimes when I feel myself slipping into limiting thoughts, anxiety or old-line thinking, I see my mind become a large White Board or screen devoid of words or feelings. I then concentrate on the White Board for maybe five seconds. Instead of fighting my thoughts and feelings into submission in order to bounce back to the present, I paste words of encouragement on my White Board, such as: My reality is *my* definition; I live in a safe universe; I choose a new probability; I create everything I see; _____is no longer an option; I am free to be me; My future includes_____; The point of power is NOW.

During my early days of metaphysics while employed by Apple Computer, and when my goal was freedom through money, I would slap the words, "I'm wealthy and free," on my White Board intermittently throughout my day. I did it as an affirmation, but perhaps more as a way of stopping the doubts that would arise from time to time. When you fill your mind with white and words of wisdom, there is no room for anything else—and so you return to the now instead of lingering in the past, and the now is your point of power.

For me, the White Board has become an effective way of utilizing the present moment, and I use it as the starting point for much of my inner work. Once my mind becomes a White Board, then I'm ready to do whatever it is I'm working on at the time, whether it is to launch into a visualization scene, alter beliefs or talk to my inner self.

Mixing Imaging and Words

An extension of the White Board technique combines words and activity. Sometimes I start with my words of choice and then segue into seeing a scene that brings them alive. One time, for instance, Stan and I wanted to sell some undeveloped land we owned. Stan handled the technical details and I did my part through imaging. First on my White Board I saw the words, "The land sold!" I held the phrase in place while I said the words in my mind several times. Then the White Board became a screen for the living enactment of the words. There Stan and I were, standing on the land, laughing and discussing the signed contract of sale in our hands, so happy to have brought the event to a successful conclusion. And that's eventually what happened.

By the way, Seth says it doesn't matter whether we use words or images for our mind's projections. Either will work. So, if you don't feel at ease with your visualization skills, don't worry. Simply run the words that reflect your desire through your mind. Get a sense of what you really want to accomplish, and let the excitement of the words develop. Remember, it's really the emotion generated by consciousness that starts the emission of electromagnetic energy units. Thought triggers emotion, but emotion is the ingredient of strength when discussing how reality is created.

Dear Diary

I especially enjoy this technique for programming the future with what I want to experience, because it's relatively quick, always fun, and I don't have to be in an altered state to do it. Like the exercise above, it mixes words and images.

I pretend I'm my future self writing in her diary about an event that she's remembering from her past—or what is to become *my* future. I start by saying, "Dear Diary," and I see the words handwritten across the screen of my mind. Next I "write" a phrase such as, "You'll never guess what happened yesterday!" Then I go on to describe with excitement an event that occurred in my future self's past, but is yet to enter my reality. I've switched from writing in the diary to visualizing the scene by now, but I keep up the verbal patter in the background. My immediate self, the one in the present, laces the now with feelings of excitement and conviction that the event will come to pass.

Living the Half Bubble

Once you feel confident of your expertise in creating vivid visual images, try this process. See yourself within a bubble that extends from the point of peripheral vision of your left eye to the farthest point of peripheral vision of the right eye. In essence, you are within a half bubble. Now divide the half bubble into equal sections. Clockwise from the left, section one holds a picture of your future home as you've defined it, bursting with feelings of abundance and fulfillment; section two has a rendition of the Bank of You, bulging with gold coins and bills coming out of the roof and windows; section three denotes a scene that symbolizes your career or life's focus, pulsating with vibrancy and success; and section four shows you surrounded by people you love and trust, goodwill flowing freely between all.

If the scenes I've described aren't ones you desire to actualize—or you already have them in place in physical reality—substitute others of choice. How about a white BMW? An Australian vacation? Winning a coveted award? You're the artist and the creator, so have fun designing your new life.

Seeing the Camouflage

To help sense the flexibility of this reality, to really grasp that time, space and matter are illusion or camouflage, try this. Sit quietly in a room in your home. Look at a particular object, such as a dresser or wood stove. Study its shape and size, get a sense of its solidness. Now glance around and tell yourself that everything you see looks real, but it is only camouflage patterns of other things, things found in the inner reality. Tell yourself you're looking at idea constructions made physical.

Now, start to see everything as consciousness which has allowed itself to be molded into shapes. See the items start to become less solid, more crafted of ever-moving molecules with obvious space between them. Study an object and "see" through it as though it's made of mist. Now do the same thing to the walls of your room, and the walls of your house, until there is no solid structure at all, simply consciousness within consciousness.

Then, if you wish to continue, sense an antique chest or piece of furniture directly ahead of you. See it start to take on form and shape from the mist of consciousness, defying time and space. See it solidify into a definite object, as "real" as your own furniture.

Know that you are the sculptor that molds consciousness into objects, that you select the space in which they will appear and the time in which they find themselves.

And then know this for an ancient truth, because it is.

Finding Beliefs

To find beliefs takes first an awareness of their character and then time and effort applied to identifying the ones you consider limiting, and that's what was discussed in chapter 5. Hopefully, that information was helpful in opening your mind to beliefs in general, and your personal ones in particular. Now here are some other suggestions for finding limiting beliefs, the first being one I used heavily in my beginning years of metaphysics and still find extremely beneficial.

Take out a notebook. Select the area of your life you want to analyze and write it at the top of a blank page. Now write what you're thinking about the subject, either in prose or bullet items. Note whatever comes to mind. Write in short phrases, without worrying about grammar. Cover as many facets as possible, such as your thoughts, some events that have occurred, and your feelings.

After you have listed the contents of your conscious mind as it pertains to your chosen subject, quietly, slowly review what you have written. Relax and let intuitive information surface. Soon the overriding beliefs that frame the situation will become apparent. When you're through, or even at a later time, review your writings and try to develop simple statements that summarize what you have written. Your summary will give you a good handle on your beliefs.

Or, try this. Write yourself a letter. Describe recent unsettling events in your life and how you feel about them. Talk about why they hit you like they did, and ask yourself the question, "Why would I have participated in such an event?" Then ask yourself why *anyone* would have participated in that type of situation.

Compare your responses and see if, between the two of them, you receive new insights into how and why you put that scenario into place.

Here's another technique for finding beliefs. Create a list of negative emotions that you have felt at one time or another. Then select a subject of choice; for instance, your job. Bring each emotion into your mind individually and then place it in the context of your work. Let's say the emotion is depression. What about your job makes your feel depressed, if it does? Write your responses on paper. You'll soon end up with a list of thoughts surrounding the subject of your livelihood—and those thoughts will summarize your beliefs.

The following are some reflections of a person's beliefs. Think about their relationship to all facets of your life; they will guide you to some interesting insights.

> Emotions; actions; reactions; memories; body; possessions; thoughts of future; home and work environments; internal chatter; guilts; prejudices; fears; career; political position; friends; life philosophy.

Changing Beliefs

So, how *do* we change beliefs? The easiest way is simply to let them go. Make a conscious choice not to believe them any longer. It really can be that simple. But most of us aren't ready to accept that at first, so we need processes and techniques to use. We can design our own, or use ones developed by others, but no technique will work unless we *believe* in it.

Beliefs enter our life through self-hypnosis, so we can use the same tool to get rid of them. Seth suggests that for five or ten minutes a day, at most, we "use natural hypnosis as a method of accepting desired new beliefs." He says to concentrate our attention as vividly as possible on one statement of desire, and keep repeating it to ourselves as we imagine its outcome. Whether we say the statement aloud while visualizing or mentally repeat it doesn't matter. The repetition is important, though, because it literally activates biological and psychic patterns that then come to pass. A light altered state is helpful for such an exercise, since it puts us in a more focused mind-set naturally.

A twist to the above suggestion is this: Project your White Board into your mind, and see an undesirable belief written on it. Slash a large black X through it, and erase its image off the Board. Then see a new supportive belief appear in its place. Focus on the new belief, and, all the while, build the emotion that reflects the belief (i.e., happiness, excitement, love, contentment). Do this with repetition, as Seth suggests.

Here's another technique for changing beliefs. Since beliefs are reinforced by normal inner talking, we can use the same process to our advantage by selecting our chatter. We can become our own conscious hypnotist and insert repetitive information into our minds throughout the day. One way is to select a belief you want to insert into your psyche, and about every half hour or so, stop what you're doing and simply stare into space. Say your desired belief, get the feelings moving around it, repeat it several times and then drop it. It helps to write the belief on a piece of paper that is always in view, so when you're ready to start your exercise you can kick it off by first studying the slip of paper.

In *Beyond the Winning Streak*, I outlined a visualization I've used for years for belief removal. It entails seeing your limiting beliefs as pillars of stone that you eventually vaporize with the power of your thought. Visualization is, in fact, an excellent method of removing unwanted beliefs and inserting ones you'd rather experience. Here's a good one for your repertoire.

Picture yourself at a fork in the road. The path to your left is dark and depressing. Several yards down that path is a White Board. On it are written the limiting beliefs you want to eliminate. The path to your right is brightly lit, alive with promise and excitement. The air tingles with it. It's the path you will walk once the limiting beliefs are eliminated. As you stand at the fork viewing each of the probable paths, make the conscious choice to select the path to the right. That decision starts a process of change. See the words on the White Board to your left dissolve into nothingness, no longer part of your reality. The elimination of the scene closes down the probability it represents.

Now walk to the right and place your feet on the path leading to your new future. There you are up ahead, having a splendidly good time living your life of choice. See the future as you've defined it, with all the satisfaction and joy you expect to experience. The "you" in that event is literally the future you. Put all the positive emotion and feeling that you can muster into the new life's enactment. Imagine it with the vividness of physical reality. To end the scene, see yourself joyfully jumping up into space, head thrown back, arms above your head, knees bent. You are absolutely certain that you have succeeded in creating what you want. *Feel it; know it.*

Keep in mind that the visualized future scene may not be created in your reality exactly as you picture it. What will happen, though, is that the *feelings* you project into your future will wash over the event, coloring its outcome to your liking.

Accentuate the Positive

"In all such situations, it is highly important that you do not concentrate your main attention in that area of experience with which you are least satisfied. This acts as a deepening of hypnotic suggestion. Just reminding yourself of your other accomplishments will by <u>itself</u> operate in a constructive fashion, even if nothing else is done."[2] This Seth quote speaks worlds of words to us. While a book such as this one is oriented toward identifying and eliminating the negative, we must not forget to accentuate the positive, as the song goes.

When you start your search for beliefs, you'll stumble upon all types, not just ones you wish to change. Make a note of the positive ones that influence your life. Keep a running list of the beliefs that support you in what you're attempting to accomplish. Peruse this list often. Get a sense that these beliefs should be taken very seriously, in that they are extremely important to creating your future. And, at the same time, pat yourself on the back for having solidified them in your psyche in the first place. You did it, you know; it's your success you're staring at when you peruse your list. Give yourself some credit. Build the belief that it wasn't so difficult to cultivate these positive beliefs, and know you can do it just as easily with your "less fortunate" ones.

A Caution Flag on Beliefs

After all is said and done on finding beliefs, after all is said about them being the golden rule that forms reality, I raise a word of caution. Don't do what I did: Don't give the *idea* of beliefs too much of your power. Yes, they are power hitters; yes, you need to pay attention to them, find them, change them. Oh, yes. But they *are* changeable. They *are* breakable. They *are not* permanent. The power of my belief in the power of my beliefs was a trying situation, and one that took up much of my time. What a relief it finally was to see the situation clearly. It broke the paralysis I'd placed on portions of my life because I became free to let the limiting beliefs go with ease, sometimes at will. Not that all my life is peaches and cream, by any means, and some of my old beliefs hold on with tenacity. But I'm learning, and some day I'll break the belief that some of my old beliefs hold on with tenacity, and then I'll breathe a final sigh of relief and be on my way.

Becoming Aware of Background Thought

It's amazing how our background thoughts take over when we allow them to go unnoticed. For years we've bracketed our days within habits of thought that do us no justice. They're the ones that quietly tell us how stupid our last decision was, but it's nothing unusual, our stupid decisions are the norm; that we're so tired we can't possibly lead a productive day; that life sure is a bitch, just not much fun any more; that most people are not trustworthy; that, Oh, God, how are we going to get through another week on our job, let alone years? They're the negative thoughts we accept as our right to think. They're the ones that allow us to criticize others mentally when we'd die before we'd do it openly. They're the ones we think about the "real" way we view ourselves and our foibles, when there is no way on earth we'd talk of such things to another soul. They're the thoughts we express on the inside because we feel that's where they'll stay.

Wrong. None of our thoughts are hidden or secret. Our inner selves know them well, and build our next moments based upon them. These thoughts go unnoticed by us exactly because they are in background mode. While we're writing the last line of our weekly report, waiting for our next customer to enter the store, lying on the beach in the heat of summer, flying the friendly skies between Los Angeles and Boston, lines of thought lazily float through our minds, no big deal. Well, yes they are, if what they're creating isn't to our liking or benefit.

Habits of thought take on other forms, also, and in some ways these may become more important to recognize. They direct large areas of our existence because they are patterns of thought about our life that go unnoticed simply because they are full-blown assumptions—and so hide within our everyday thinking unquestioned. For instance, what assumptions have you made about the condition of your aging body? Do you see yourself growing older and meeting the supposed diseases of the aged? Do you expect wrinkles by fifty? Do you assume loss of hearing will occur with age? Do you assume you have a high chance of diabetes because others in your family have the problem? Now, what are your habits of thought about your financial status, love life, opportunities, relationships, skills, school work, athletic abilities, etc., etc.?

Here's a technique for becoming aware of your background thoughts. Every half hour or so stop what you're doing and jot in your notebook what you can remember of your thinking since your last entry. Don't spend great amounts of time trying to dredge up the thoughts; don't worry, they'll be back in some form if they are habitual enough. The important thing is to start to realize just how negative you can be without obvious awareness. Do this little exercise for a week and you'll probably never go back to not consciously monitoring your thoughts. You'll be so shocked at the end of your trial week that you'll never let your inner chatter get so sloppy again.

Altering an Event Before It Enters Physical Reality

You have an appointment with your tax person; you expect the results to be depressing based on "facts" of which you are aware. You have been having conflicts with a co-worker; you know an altercation is imminent. Your car is in for service; you suspect the bill will be much higher than you can afford.

These probable events feel very solid to you because you have physical facts already in hand that suggest a definite outcome will manifest in your future. Sure, these events are still in the field of probabilities, but something tells you there's a good chance of them entering your life. What to do? Change their outcome through imaging.

Once again create a fork in the road. But this time on the left, picture the scene as you think it might occur. Feel the depression, the fear, the feeling of helplessness, the anger that you expect will take place. See it in living color, with all its hopelessness—and then dissolve it. To the right visualize the scene or result that you want to create, and walk into it. Make sure you place yourself in the event. See the happiness on your face, the relief, the thankfulness that it turned out so well after all. Dwell on the great feeling of joy. Work the scene in your visualization until you feel very much at ease with its outcome. Then let it go until the next day when you will repeat the same scenario, and continue repeating it day after day until the modified event is met in time.

In some situations there's not enough time to work through the longer suggestions mentioned here. What works well as an alternative is to quiet your mind as quickly as possible, and then concentrate only on the positive scene. Picture it clearly in your mind's eye. See the faces of the participants break into smiles, picture everyone shaking hands. See a mist of understanding swirl around the people. Maybe have everyone get a hug or form a circle holding hands. The point is to project goodwill out into your future, so you can walk into it when the time comes.

It's always more powerful to get to the beliefs that will cause the negative future scene to take place, before altering it with visualization. So it's recommended that over a period of several days, if there is time, you apply yourself to belief work to discover why you're in the distracting situation in the first place.

Altering the Body

"You hypnotize your very nerves, and the cells within your body, for they will react as you _expect_ them to react, and the beliefs of your conscious mind are followed in degree by all portions of the self down to the smallest atom and molecule. The large events of your life, your interactions with others, including the habitual workings of the most minute physical events within your body—all of this follows your conscious belief."[3]

Basically, the body is no more than an extension of the mind. There is much talk about the mind-body connection nowadays, but if we were to back up into consciousness, where nothing is yet solidified into matter, we'd see that the mind sets the body's blueprint into motion, brings it to fruition at birth and cradles it as a physical extension of itself. But the body is _always part of the mind_. So, more accurately, it can be said that the body is an extension of the mind.

Another bout of semantics? Not when you're attempting to heal a living organism which you think (hope?) can be influenced by the mind. Of course it can be! It _is_ the mind, or a portion of it.

You don't have to be concerned one iota about the workings of the body in order to heal yourself. You don't have to know medical terms, scientific theories, bone structure or virus movement. They are irrelevant to the healing process. All you have to do is work within the mind to make changes occur. In fact, that's the *only* method of changing bodily conditions, of any sort. You make up your mind to bring change into your world, and you select your system of choice, be it conscious creation or Western medicine. Neither is superior to the other. After all, whatever stops the pain is the bottom line we seek.

Here's a little aside, a very interesting one, I think. According to Seth, when we heal ourselves, what we've actually done is select a new probability in the moment and insert it into our past, and that probability is one where we had no physical problem. As a result, that healthy probability is met now, in our life. In other words, we really don't move forward through time to reach a place of health; we simply select a probability that suits our present desires, insert it into the past—and in comes a healthy body.

So, one method of healing is this: See your body "backing up" through time to a scene where you were without today's problem. Bring that person into clear focus, see the body at ease, with things on its mind other than health issues—because there are none in that probability. Now superimpose the past you over today's you, and feel the vitality of that body seep into the moment, flooding your awareness, becoming your awareness. Hold that picture for as long as you can, then let it go for awhile. Do the same process several times throughout the day for as long as necessary.

You can also simply reject the illness condition from your reality. Say, "This is no longer an option," and mean it; then get on with your day without fueling the problem through negative thoughts.

The visualizations for healing are endless, and rather well covered in many books on the market. You, however, are the director of your play, so it's best you select the ingredients that feel right to you for your healing, and use them lavishly. Some people may want to go within the body to the point of pain, and work their mind magic on that specific area. Others may use focused light or energy, if they believe in those processes. It really doesn't matter what you choose. Every single one of the techniques you can conjure up, from the intake of medicine to conscious visual manipulations, are all played out in your mind, anyway, and that's where their success lies.

To end this section on the body, here's an interesting thought. When does an illness actually start? For instance, my sister owns a delicatessen, and one of her workers was exposed to hepatitis. The health authorities said the incubation period for the virus was three weeks. So, after taking suggested precautions, my sister settled in to see what would happen to her worker. At the end of the waiting period, the worker did indeed test positive to the disease.

The question is, when did the creation of that illness happen? Did it start three weeks earlier, or did it happen in the spacious present, made to look like it conformed to the timetables of science? Was my sister's employee stricken with a disease she could not easily escape because of its highly infectious nature, or did she mull over the decision on another level of consciousness, think about the repercussions in her life, and finally decide to actualize it in physicality? You know what Seth would say.

Mind-Communicating With Your Inner Self

When I need an answer from my inner self, at times I want it immediately. I know it will show up in physical reality sooner or later once I ask for it, but sometimes sooner is better than later. So I've designed a technique for consciously getting a response quickly, and once again it involves my White Board. In the beginning days of developing my ability to listen for my inner self's words, I'd go into a rather deep altered state of consciousness. Eventually I gravitated to using a light altered state, and now I'll either use that state or simply quiet my mind while wide awake.

I'll ask my question when I feel very still, and then picture my White Board. I make an effort to keep my mind clear of extraneous thoughts and emotion. To facilitate this, I see a fine mist being pushed from the center of the White Board in all directions, as though blown by a hose of air, leaving its surface sparkling clear. I'll do this several times while I'm asking my question, and then I'll stop all action and wait for a response.

Soon my answer will start to form on the White Board. It will be hazy at first, but then develop form rather quickly. It's not like it's magic-marker crisp, but usually it will have some substance, albeit nebulous at times. The *sense* of the word or words also comes through most of the time; that is, I hear my mind echoing the words as quiet far-away thoughts, while the image of the answer is still on the board.

If you're new to using an approach such as this to talk to your inner self, I'd suggest you start with questions that require a yes/no answer. After a while, you'll progress to requesting longer responses, but in the beginning it seems easier to start more simply. Actually, I seldom see answers in the form of long sentences on the board. I'm pretty good at yes/no responses to my questions, but I tend to "hear" the longer answers, seemingly coming from the lower right side of my mind as quiet far-away thoughts.

There's a downside to this approach of direct communication. It's rather easy for our mind to color what we're hearing, based on different factors (the strength of our belief in the subject at hand, our emotions of the moment, our desire for a specific outcome, etc.). For instance, one time I asked for the percentage of probability that a certain event would occur. I got 95 percent. At first I was ecstatic, but then grew uneasy about the answer. It sounded almost too pat, too confident based on the situation. Stan and I'd been playing with probabilities and verifying their outcomes for awhile, and something didn't jibe. The Committee later confirmed that I had indeed colored the answer: It was actually 76 percent.

The most natural mode of communication, and the clearest in terms of undistorted information, comes through intuition, impulse and insight. We don't have time to color the responses because we are not expecting them...and so do not set the stage to interfere with the answer. It's true we may not receive as precise an answer as "76 percent," but we will get a good sense of where we stand on the issue.

But I feel by exercising the inner senses through consciously requesting answers actually helps us develop our ability to hear and sense other forms of communication. And in spite of the potential distortions, I still get right-on responses much of the time. I finally decided that if I get a 95 percent, but question its validity, I'd just assume it to be correct and see what happens. Gee, what a concept.

A Psy-Time Exercise: Meeting Your Inner Self

There are other ways of directly communicating with our inner self. In fact, there are as many variations as there are people. One tool many use is meditation, or a deep altered state of consciousness. Seth calls it Psychological Time, or Psy-Time, and it's one of the inner senses. Psy-Time is a bridge from the outer world to the inner world, and according to Seth, by using it we cut down the amount of time it takes to manifest whatever we desire because we're extremely focused on our goal, with no extraneous activity to break our concentration. Therefore, our inner self hears our request loud and clear.

So, what we're going to do now is a Psy-Time exercise, the purpose of which is to put us in conscious contact with our inner self. It's designed to remove our focus from the day-to-day environment by going inward, and so assist us to more quickly manifest whatever it is we desire, from answers to material objects. Your task is to decide what it is you want to accomplish during this time and prepare yourself to present it to your inner self.

I used to do this specific exercise a lot, and I believe it helped set the stage for the emergence of the Committee on the Ouija board. Not that any preparation was necessary under certain conditions, but what the exercise did for me was to eventually change my belief into one that said direct communication was indeed possible.

For the first of the altered-state exercises offered in this book, the lead-in of relaxation and wrap-up of the return to normal consciousness will be included; they won't be repeated with the rest of the exercises to relieve redundancy. In fact, the other exercises will be presented in a more informal text style than what's presented below. You may want to put this meditation on audiotape for convenience sake.

According to Seth, we may have to repeat this type of exercise several to many times in order to achieve our goal, depending on what the goal is and how soon we'll allow it to manifest. What you request may or may not show up in your reality immediately. Sometimes you might get the information as a thought or impression right away, but at times it may not come to you for several days. Just know it will show up sooner or later, though.

Sure, that newspaper article you happen to read that answers the question posed to your inner self is a coincidence. Surely the words to a song long forgotten that spring to mind—and happen to hold the solution you requested in Psy-Time—is a coincidence. Yeah, and your dream two nights after meditation, the one that outlined the direction you sought, was a coincidence, too.

Well, here's to many wonderful coincidences!

Just let your eyelids close, and rest...
let all your facial muscles relax...
take a deep breath and hold it...
count from one to three
and then let out the breath...
and let...your...body relax

Just let your body sink down and relax...
relaxing...just letting go...
Let yourself feel the peace and tranquillity
that is all around you...that is within...

Just relaxing...letting go...
taking another deep breath
and slowly letting it out...
Feel that comfortable...peaceful...tranquil
state of mind and body...

Listen gently to the distant sound of the waves...
and let your mind...drift...and flow...
with the distant...sound of the waves...

Now picture yourself sitting
in a large, peaceful room,
comfortable with your surroundings,
feeling great contentment...
Slowly, very slowly, arise from your chair
and start walking across the room...

Feel your feet press against the floor...
Reach out and touch a lovely pink rose
in a black vase halfway to the door
you are heading toward
See the intensity of its color...
feel the softness of a petal

As you resume your slow walk,
know that on the other side of that door
is the special place in the universe
where all begins...know it as home
Know it as the place where your inner self resides

Know that when you open the door
you will see an infinity of velvet black softness
studded with tiny glittering sparks of light
with softly muted wisps of color
gently swirling about...

> *Now let these words become your words...*
> My mind is quieting
> My mind is quieting
> as I walk to the threshold
> of the universe
>
> As I open the door
> and step from my room
> of conscious thought
> into the place where all begins,
> I feel the comfort and
> peacefulness of home surround me
>
> A bright white light is moving
> toward me, growing in
> brilliance as it approaches
> I welcome it with joy and awe
> I open my arms to the
> light of universal love
>
> It surrounds me...
> I absorb the light...
> *I become the light...*
>
> Free of my body I am one with
> my inner self...
> I am filled with joy and expectation!
> **I *AM* MY INNER SELF**...

Now tell your inner self
what it is you came for
Listen to what it says to you,
watch for movement, color, impressions
Intuitively feel and hear the response from
your inner self to your need or desire
(note: give yourself five to twenty minutes of quiet time here)

Now let go of the question
let go of the thought...
let go of the thinking
Just let go and relax...just relax

And know without a doubt
that you have started the creative process
of manifesting whatever it is
you have discussed with your inner self...

Know, *know* that *you* are the creator
of all success...and your inner self
is your constant advisor
Know also that you have now opened
intuitive channels between you and
your inner self, channels you can
now develop with ease

Coming back...coming back now...
Feel yourself coming back now...
Gently...easily...coming back...

Begin to feel the physical body...
Feel the physical body...
Get a sense of it...

And then, on the count of three
your eyes will open and you will be
wide awake, feeling relaxed
comfortable and refreshed in every way...
remembering all that you have
experienced with your inner self...
One...two...three...

Flexing Our Inner Senses

Seth says the inner senses are channels that provide communication between various dimensions of existence, and that it is up to us to apply our minds to using them. What we have been doing throughout this chapter is not only to build awareness of our inner senses, but to learn to consciously use them to our advantage. They are there for us, whether we know it or not and for whatever purpose we request.

Processes, programs, techniques and exercises are all excellent tools for flexing the muscles of our inner senses, but that's all they are. They're temporary assists, but they're not mandatory. Some day none of us will need such things because we will have outgrown their helpfulness. We'll be so sure of our spot in simultaneous time and all it implies, and so comfortable with our creative power and ability to use our inner senses naturally, that we'll move through life without having to give a single thought to using boosters. But for now, they're very welcomed and appreciated.

And, on that note, we'll continue into the next chapter with other (temporary) exercises of choice, ones specifically directed toward changing the past and selecting the future, the purview of magicians and masters in days gone by—and now our territory.

8

*As far as you are concerned the present is your point of action, fo-
cus and power, and from that point of volition you form both
your future and past. Realizing this, you will understand that
you are not at the mercy of a past over which you have no control.*
—Seth, **The Nature of Personal Reality,** *Session 654*

Time Sculpting

In Jane Roberts' wonderful novel, *Oversoul Seven and the Museum
of Time,* the man who was "scheduled" to uncover and write the
Codicils (a new model for civilization) was a dentist from the
1890s, Dr. George Brainbridge. It seems Dr. George secretly prac-
ticed out-of-body experiments, either by sniffing laughing gas or
consciously preparing for an altered state of consciousness. When
Oversoul Seven enters the 20th century in the time of Dr. George's
grandson to check on the progress of the Codicils, he finds they
haven't yet been discovered—and he becomes frantic with concern.

At one point, Cypress, Seven's oversoul, tells him, "It's really
quite simple. Dr. George has to find the Codicils in the 25th century museum (while out of body), and write them down in his
journal in the 1890s so that his grandson can find them in the attic
in the 20th century and put them on microfilm in the bomb shelter.

Then they can be found by Monarch in the 25th century, as they *are* in that probable future. Nothing could be simpler."

If we were to join Cypress and Oversoul Seven outside time and space where this conversation took place, I'm sure the inter-action of moments, years and lifetimes would look simple to us, too. We'd see the flexibility of the universe in all its brilliance, all its logic. We'd finally grasp simultaneous time and creation, and understand why events are always open to revision and never fi-nalized.

But since we've chosen to become pinpoints of consciousness in linear time for the moment, we must plug away at teaching our-selves these new ideas in the face of "facts" that scream otherwise. Books such as Seth's and Jane's help enormously, but in the end it gets down to each of us believing the information enough to allow ourselves to play with it. We need to see how change occurs when we utilize the spacious present instead of working within the out-line of linear time. Seth says his job is to open our eyes; then surely ours must be to integrate this mind-boggling information so thor-oughly into our belief systems that there is no doubt in our minds whatsoever as to the way the universe functions.

Actually, that's the real purpose behind conscious creation. You might have thought it was to materialize the winning lottery ticket, but not so. It's to see physical reality for what it is, so we can bring abundance in all things into our lives, not just a mar-velous event here and there. So, within this chapter we will further explore the ways and means of selecting new probabilities to ex-perience by working with all-important time.

Behind the Scenes of Life

When I first started reading the Seth books, I saw no practical application of simultaneous time to everyday life, so while I found it fascinating in theory, it stayed just that. The cosmic joke was on me, though, because there is no way to separate simultaneous time from physical life. It's at the core of the creation process. Nothing would make sense in this universe, or any other, if time was not happening at once.

Time has to be adjustable in order for All That Is to experience unpredictability, which is one of its traits. All That Is has the ingrained ability to experience every nuance of probability possible—and so do we, as portions of It—and that's what keeps the universe and life from becoming stagnant. Anything can change at any time, past, present or future, and this must be so in order for creation to continuously occur.

I kept reading of the spacious present and probabilities sprinkled throughout the Seth/Jane books, and finally, glimmers of their significance started to penetrate my obtuseness. How, I began to wonder, was it that I could command a parking place simply by visualizing it? What if none of the people presently parked in front of the post office wanted to leave when I arrived? What if there were four cars idling their engines in front of me as their drivers also awaited their turn at a parking place? Did I "force" someone to leave the post office before completing their business in order for my visualization to be actualized? Did I "force" the four drivers to give up in disgust and leave the vicinity in order for me to get my parking place? Was I in competition with these people, and was I the winner because I knew a trick they didn't?

The answers to how a parking place is created are the same answers to how anything is. Consciousness sets a goal through focus and intent. The thoughts and emotion behind the intent draw from the field of probabilities outside time and space one that matches the goal. If the intent is not quite strong enough, the probability never reaches actualization in physical reality, but is played out somewhere else. If the intent is sufficient and mental blockages are at a minimum, the probability is inserted into the individual's space continuum as a polished event.

One of the keys here is the "individual's space continuum." I choose my probabilities and play them out in my space continuum, as you do in yours. The reason we're not at odds over who wins is that we both have probabilities where we get a parking place. Each person in the city does, in fact. And since our lives are played out in separate space continuums, it all works beautifully. We all win, if we want to. This, in fact, is why we don't share a joint reality. Only one could win at a time if there were only one space continuum for all people, and yet as a literal part of All That Is we have the ability to create whatever we choose, when we choose it. So one slice of space assigned to all wouldn't work.

I have infinite active probabilities around this infamous parking place, any in which I could participate as surely as the one I finally choose to make happen. It doesn't mean the others are any less real; they simply aren't chosen for insertion into my space continuum. You come and play in my arena if you choose to "lend" me one of your probabilities where you show up in my life. You also play in many other space continuums where different stories are being unfolded. But the main focus of your consciousness takes place in your own space continuum, because that's the life you are creating with the most intensity in the 20th century.

True, there is much in common between what's happening in our space continuums. When we decided to be born in the 20th century, we agreed to keep much of our individual realities in alignment with what our contemporaries see, and we do this through telepathy. We usually agree on world events, history, geography, etc., because those idea constructions come with the territory, so to speak. The common elements we share form the playing field of 20th century life and act as a stage for our private life's creations. But within that structure, I get to design my life according to my rules. And that includes consciously changing my past and selecting my future by sprinkling new probabilities throughout my space continuum in the spacious present.

Changing Trauma to Drama

In the forties, tuberculosis was still very much a dreaded killer disease. By 1950, at the tail end of my second grade of grammar school, my father was released from a TB sanitarium after having spent six years there, on and off, mostly on, and losing a lung and many ribs to the surgeon's efforts to save him. My mother collected my three sisters and me from various temporary housing around the country where we'd spent the better part of five years while she had worked herself to desperation trying to support four small children and a very sick husband.

When Dad was released from the sanitarium, my mother, a registered nurse, brought us together in a new town where she could be within walking distance of her job at a local hospital. Our new home was a tiny one-and-a-half bedroom apartment over a dilapidated garage whose rickety entrance staircased off a back alley. The problem arose for me, a sensitive, shy seven-year-old, in the fact that the dilapidated garage was on the back grounds of a splendid house on a street of elegant homes lining the Detroit River, some of which boasted maids or housekeepers. The town seemed overflowing with abundance, its lovely churches on shady streets and children with shiny patent leather shoes and ironed clothing in stark contrast to what I knew of the world.

As long as my new school friends didn't know the condition of our housing, I felt safe. But one day when I was alone in the apartment, two classmates came for an unexpected visit. My shock was traumatic. When I heard their feet on the squeaky staircase and their childish voices, I dropped behind a chair in the living room, hidden from the view of the open door. My friends knocked and called my name. I hyperventilated. As they turned to descend into the alley, they talked about our dump of a home, using language only kids can conjure up.

My life changed in that moment. I entered a probability that verified assumptions I held about myself that had no validity whatsoever. I heaped the old beliefs with new ones about my self-worth, my place in life and my apartness, that helped shape my life for years to come. I didn't see them as beliefs, I saw them as truths. I battled with those truths until recently, winning some skirmishes, losing others. I knew when I started reading the Seth material that I had to address my limiting beliefs once and for all, because they placed a lid on my potential just as tightly as a the screwed-down top of a Bell jar.

Seth gave me knowledge. He told me there are many probabilities surrounding each event I ever experience, and any could have been chosen by me for actualization that day. I simply aligned with the one I did based on my beliefs and desires of the moment. Looked at neutrally, as all events could be, it was simply the expression of my thoughts, attitudes and feelings of the time. Other players came into my script, acting out their parts with so much conviction that even I believed them—and I'm the one who not only wrote them into my play, but directed the scene and became the audience who cried at curtain fall.

But, according to Seth, our directorship is open-ended, meaning we can rethink a scene whenever we choose and alter its significance dramatically. We can take a stumbling block to our happiness or fulfillment and make it the growth path to our future. Seth says, "The fact remains that there are probable past events that 'can still happen' within your personal previous experience. A new event can literally be born in the past—now....A new belief in the present can cause changes in the past....When you alter your beliefs today you also reprogram your past."[1] At another point he says, "To rid yourself of annoying restrictions then...you re-pattern your past from the present."[2]

So, here's what I did, and it may have been the most important process of my life. In an altered state of consciousness, or Psy-Time, I re-created the scene and played out the event just as it had occurred, except I inserted today's self into the picture. Today's "me" watched from across the room as strong emotion coursed through my seven-year-old self. Then, after the other children had departed, I sat on the couch and waited for my younger self to become aware of me. Her reaction when she noticed me was shyness, but when I beckoned her to the couch, she joined me.

Then we had a heart-to-heart talk. She listened intently while I told her that her beliefs, beliefs she just may have brought into this life with her, shaped that event. And I told her those beliefs didn't particularly hold any power over her; it was only her *belief* in their power that did. I told her she was quite capable of altering that event by consciously choosing another probability to experience.

Then I told her I was her future self, and I talked about some of the more special things we'd accomplished in our life, and that we had two fine children and a loving mate and a nice home. She smiled. She was starting to grasp that life didn't end with that latest painful event, that it continued and indeed offered some choice morsels of love, security and happiness.

Then we laid a plan. She would create an instant replay of that event, but this time the ending would change—because she would change. She'd still live off the alley over a garage, but she'd be proud of it. She'd be proud of what her parents had been able to accomplish given their circumstances. She'd be pleased that they had moved her into a town where she could learn so much, such as how prosperous people acted, and dressed and talked, and how they seemed to assume they had a right to the good things in life. And she would assume she had those same rights, because certainly she did.

So, here come the kids trooping up the creaky stairs once again. She hears them and, with anticipation in her step, she reaches the door at the same time as they do. She greets them happily and asks them to come in. Her new friends from school thought enough of her to come for a visit, and she's thrilled. Her home is not an issue with them because it isn't with her. They talk awhile, and then the children head home, glad to have spent time with the new girl in town.

As soon as they leave, she and I whoop for joy. We've done it! We've changed the past by changing probabilities by changing our beliefs. And now the frosting on the cake: in walks *our* future self. She's laughing and full of congratulations. We all sit down and talk. She tells us what's happening in her life, about her home and career, about her happiness and how our changing made it all possible. We, her past selves, sit there, excited with the picture she paints of our future, because it is indeed wonderful.

I did this Psy-Time exercise over a period of a few weeks. It was never the same in that it took on its own character each time, but the result was always a feeling of freedom from limiting beliefs and a wide-open future just waiting to be experienced.

How do I know I altered the past? At first I wasn't sure. Not that it mattered, particularly, because I sensed movement and change within myself. But then during a seminar Stan and I were conducting, someone asked me that question. Almost instantly I had my answer, because the new ending to the event immediately flashed into my mind, remembered *before* the original one. My first reaction to the question was one of ease with the outcome. And then I knew that, in my field of probabilities, I had given it more strength, more intensity than the original ending. The other one was still there, but now it was merely dress rehearsal to the grand opening night.

Seth says, in this synthesis of quotes: "Because events do not exist in the concrete, done-and-finished versions about which you have been taught, then memory must also be a different story. You must remember the creativity and the open-ended nature of events ....A root goes out in all directions. Events do also. But the roots of events go through your past, present, and future....Simultaneously, each of your past and future selves dwells in their own way now..."[3]

Preparations for Change

We can use imagination to alter past events. Since there are no consecutive moments, how we view our past right now creates it in that mold. Seth says for us to remember a particular event that greatly disturbed us, then to imagine it not simply wiped out, but replaced by another event of more beneficial nature. This must be done with great vividness and emotional validity, and many times. It is not a self-deception, he assures us. The new event that we choose will automatically be a probable event which did in fact happen, though it is not the event we selected to perceive in our given probable past. Seth says, "Telepathically, if the process is done correctly, your idea will also affect any people who were connected with the original event, though they can choose to reject as well as accept your version."[4]

So, it's your turn to re-create your past. The next Psy-Time exercise is very similar to the technique I used with my past self and is designed for you to tape record for your use, if desired. I've chosen to use the words him and his as designators of the past self. Before you go any further, select a past event you want to alter. Get clear in your mind what you want the new outcome to be, or the feelings you'd rather experience around the event, and then assume what you are about to undertake will, of course, happen.

So, get comfortable, relax and prepare to alter your past—and open your future.

A Psy-Time Exercise: Changing the Past

Now, see your past self in the setting where a previous painful or unsettling event is about to recur. See him simply waiting to start the action, as though an actor in a play. The you of today should be in the background, ready to watch the drama unfold, but unnoticed by your past self. Clearly see the props, costumes and scenery your past self has chosen for this event.

All right, let the scene roll just as it happened, with the you of today being the unseen observer. Let your past self act out his part, but the emotion of the time doesn't have to be as deep as it was then, especially if it was extremely painful. Watch your past self almost clinically to see his reaction to what is occurring.

When it's over and your past self is alone again, make it known to him that you are nearby. Have him come sit by you on whatever props fit the scene. Tell him that you are his future self,

here to assist in rewriting that event. Tell your past self it was beliefs that caused the painful experience and beliefs that can
change it. Ask him what beliefs he thinks were behind the structure of such an experience, and have him think it through and then
discuss it with you.

Tell your past self he can literally redirect that event and
change its ending. Tell him he is the creator of his life, and since he
created that scene, he can re-create it. Suggest new beliefs, feelings
and attitudes that he might embrace. Give him suggestions on a
better, more constructive ending to the event. See him get excited
at the new possibilities.

Now it's time to replay the scene with a new ending. You move
to the background as your past self takes his position on the set.
Give him a thumbs-up and a nod of encouragement. Become an
observer as the event unfolds once again, but this time watch as
your past self takes control of his emotions, beliefs and attitudes,
and by so doing, radically alters the outcome of the scene. When
it's over and the last actor has left the set, you and your past self
whoop for joy! You've done it! You've altered your past by changing in the now. What excitement you both feel!

Now, into the scene walks your future self, laughing and con-
gratulating you on the freshly restructured event. Sit with your future self and have him bring you up to date on his life. Spend time
talking with your future self, hearing just how wonderful your future will be because your past has changed, thereby allowing new,
exciting future probabilities to open to you.

Say good-bye, now, to your future and past selves. Tell them
you will meet again in another time and place. Thank them both
for helping you to change into the person you've chosen to become.

Pre-Defining the Future You

Seth says, and I quote, "Now you can alter your present
through altering your past, or you can change your present from
your future. Even these manipulations must take place in your

practical-experienced present, however. Many people have at one time or another changed their present behavior in response to the advice of a "future" probable self, without even knowing they have done so."[5]

Every probable you is alive and well in the field of probabilities. It can become a matter of conscious choice as to which "future you" you choose to actualize. One way to help you manifest who you want to be in your future is to have your future self become so known to you that she takes on a life of her own. She becomes so real, through your intent and focus, that you place her into your future...automatically.

Before you start the next Psy-Time exercise, just sit quietly with notebook and pen and design the self you want to become. What would she look like? Would your future self live in the home you now occupy or in a different one? Describe it. Would your future self be in the same career or job or school as you are now? If not, what would she be doing? Would she move in a different circle of friends, be more successful than you feel you are today, be well known? Would she be more self-possessed, less afraid, more outgoing?

Get that person clearly defined by giving her dimension and scope, and then you're ready to enter Psy-Time and create your future self. What you want to accomplish with this imaging is to become so familiar with your future self that when someone asks you what you intend to do with your life, you already know—without doubt and without thinking about it—because you know you are now the past self of your very real future self.

A Psy-Time Exercise: Meeting Your Future Self

You are now on a journey into your future. Until you're told to become part of the scene, simply watch your future self as an observer. Now, see your future self at home in her living room, sitting on the sofa reading a favorite book, with a cup of tea or coffee close by. The sun is shining through the front windows, making patterns on the floor nearby.

Observe your future self closely. What does she look like? What is she wearing? See the contentment on her face, see the obvious comfort with her place in life. Watch as your future self gets up and walks across the room to a table where there sits a silver-framed photograph. Your future self picks up the photo, studies it, and smiles. It's you in the picture, and your future self stands a moment or two remembering when she was you. She sends out mental words of encouragement to you, telling you that this future of yours is not far off.

Now see today's self walk into the living room. Future self looks up and sees you. She greets you warmly and asks you to have a seat. Study your future self for a moment. See your eyes looking back at you, see your smile, your hairstyle. Pick up an object off a close-by table and feel its texture. Look around the room at the lovely artwork and nice furnishings.

The two of you start talking. Say something to your future self such as, "You look great!" Smiling, she says back to you, "Well, thanks to your efforts to change, we've come a long way." Then ask your future self what's been happening in her life lately. Have her talk expansively about her career, or the vacation upon which she is about to embark, or the new love in her life, and feel excitement at what she tells you about *your* upcoming future.

Take a walk around the house, clearly seeing at least two rooms in all their detail. Let your future self show you awards you've won, new furniture you've purchased, the gorgeous view out the living room windows, a letter from an old friend, or whatever you feel is appropriate. Ask your future self how one or two upcoming events in your "now" life went, ones that were in her past but immediate to you, and listen as she tells you how they worked out.

Now bid your future self good-bye. Tell her you're really excited by the probabilities you have seen in your future, and thank her for being there for you. Tell her you look forward to the day when you will meet again.

Drawing From the Pool of the Present

Our next exercise is a dynamic, present moment alteration of the past, with the help of several past selves, today's you and a future self. Is it really possible to change the past from the present? You bet. According to Seth, the past is open-ended, that is, it's not finished. It can be changed from the present, based on the beliefs we hold today, how we view our past and what we think we can accomplish in our future. He suggests that we think of the present as a pool of experience drawn from many sources, fed by tributaries from both the past and the future. There are an infinite number of such tributaries, or probabilities, and through our beliefs we choose from them, adjusting their currents. "The point of power is in the present, and from that moment you choose which you, and which world," as Seth reminds us.

If we constantly focus on the belief that our early background was damaging and negative, then only such experiences will flow into our present life from the past. What we need to do is offer our past selves other options to the ones they chose to activate so that our present has a richer source of positive experience to draw upon. So, let's construct our physical reality in the form of our choice by combining desire, our knowledge that the present is our point of power, and the conscious selection of probabilities.

Before you start the next Psy-Time exercise, there's a little homework to do. Review your past and choose six or seven past selves to help you in this change process. They should be ones who were hurt or saddened by certain events, or who lived through a difficult period in your life. Get a clear picture of them in your mind, because you will be asked to envision them during the exercise.

You'll also need to have identified a future self you wish to become. Either use the previous Psy-Time exercise in this book, or do it another way, but know in advance what you want out of life. Then when you're ready, just make yourself comfortable, relax and prepare to change your past—and your future.

A Psy-Time Exercise: A Meeting of Selves—
Past, Present and Future

Here you are, in a place where no time exists, where all creation happens simultaneously. It's a place outside physical reality, but one you know intimately...because it's your true home. See it as an infinity of velvet black softness studded with tiny glittering sparks of light and softly muted wisps of color gently swirling about. There, ahead of you, is a large white marble platform suspended in space, with golden steps leading to it. Walk the golden steps onto this stunning platform.

Through your inner senses, you're told that this platform is magic. It's magic because it represents your *point of power* in the universe. Feel its power emanate and surround you. Feel the magic that this power brings to you. This platform is the place from which you will manifest whatever it is you desire, the place from which you will select the probabilities that you will insert into your present reality.

Walk to the middle of the marble platform. With eyes closed and mind clear, request that your future self, the person you most desire to become, meet you in the pavilion. Focus on this thought with intensity. Now open your eyes, and there comes your future self, walking toward you, smiling in recognition. Study your future self as he or she approaches. See your eyes looking back at you, your smile, your body as it is now defined, your choice of clothing. Get a feel for your future self, what he or she sees in their world, what confidence he or she exudes. You sense that your future self feels no limitation, no fear, no constraints. It's obvious to you that he or she is at ease and comfortable with life.

And what *is* your future self's life? As you ask the question, the velvet blackness surrounding the marble platform becomes a kaleidoscope of living scenes. In amazement and excitement, you realize these scenes are ones from your upcoming life, the life that is now being led by your future self! Watch the scenes unfold, a snippet here, a more involved one there. Watch with delight as you view some of the probabilities awaiting *you* in your future.

Riding a wave of excitement, you instantly know what it is going to take to become this person, this person of your dreams. You know it means you must change your past in order to activate the probabilities that will lead you into the life of this future self.

As the panorama of your future life returns to velvet blackness, you hear a suggestion through your inner senses to gather some of your past selves together for a creation session. You close your eyes and ask six or seven of them to join you and your future self on your point-of-power platform.

Your past selves from different times and ages begin to appear. Study each of them as they arrive and take seats in a half-circle of chairs that has materialized. Acknowledge them with a nod of your head and a smile of warmth and welcome. Now, stand at the front of the group and talk to your past selves. Tell them this is a very important meeting, because together you will re-create your past so you can become the future self who now stands at your side.

Now your future self takes over. He or she talks to the group, telling your past selves that, no matter what occurred to them, the point of power is right now, and that means they can break the chains of the past simply by *consenting* to do so. With a sweep of the hand, your future self once again draws attention to the velvet blackness surrounding the platform. Out of the blackness, stretching across the canvas of infinity, appears a cosmic circle of braided light, and within that circle shines a multitude of tiny bright silver sparks. Also in the circle are brilliant stars of gold, fewer in number than the silver sparks, but larger.

Your future self tells you that each silver and gold light in the circle represents a probability that is possible within this, your current physical existence. The silver sparks, your future self says, are probabilities not presently chosen, and the brilliant stars of gold are the probabilities that are active in this present moment, ones that are most likely to become actualized, based on today's thoughts, attitudes and beliefs.

Now your future self says, "Let's have some fun. Let's take a past self who was unhappy, unsettled or hurt, and change them into one who is assured, strong and confident. Who will volunteer?" Amongst laughter, one of your past selves steps forward. This person is told to close their eyes and relax. Drawing from the deep power of this magical place in the universe, your future self projects onto this past self the qualities of strength, confidence and assurance. And, since this platform is your point of power, the changes come to pass.

"Now look!" cries your future self. "Look at the circle of probabilities!" All heads turn upward and watch in amazement at the play of lights across infinity. Some silver sparks become gold stars and former gold stars change into silver sparks, creating a dazzling display of cosmic fireworks.

"Do you understand what's happened?" your future self exclaims. "We've changed probabilities by changing our attitudes and beliefs! We've opened new possibilities in the present because we've altered our past! And that's one of the secrets to creating the future of our desire. Look at how powerful we are!" The faces of your past selves light up with understanding and excitement at what they are seeing and hearing. They now know the great power that is theirs—the power to change their life in this very moment, by changing themselves.

Now, one by one, your future self will help alter the attitudes and beliefs of each past self. As before, have a past self walk to the center of the platform. Drawing from the deep power of this magical place, your future self will project onto this past self the qualities of strength, confidence and assurance. And, since this platform is your point of power, the changes will come to pass.

As you complete your work, a cosmic sunset is created for you, a magnificent, dramatic combination of music and light. And from its depths emerge these words, burning across the brilliant universe like diamonds—*The Beginning.*

A Recipe for Success

There are certain ingredients at play when we make something happen in our life, consciously or not. Desire, combined with belief, imagination and assumption, becomes a powerful recipe for success, especially when mixed with knowledge of the power of the moment and our creative abilities. The next Psy-Time exercise combines the lot into a strong focus directed toward manifesting a specific goal in Framework 2, the psychological medium where all creation takes place.

Before you start, peruse your list of desires and objectives and choose one on which to work. Think it through very carefully so you can call up the image of the item or event with clarity when asked to do so. Also, you'll be asked to define the goal in words as well as images, so have a sentence formed that describes what you want to manifest.

This exercise uses more color and visuals than the previous ones. In some ways it's more fun because you can crank your imagination to full speed. And, from what we've learned in the Seth material, directed imagination is extremely potent. So, enjoy yourself as you start the process of actualizing your goal of choice.

A Psy-Time Exercise: Manifesting Your Desire

Welcome! Welcome on this journey to the land of magic...the land where creation takes place, the mystical, wonderful land called Framework 2. You are standing on a sun-drenched beach watching the waves of the blue-green ocean lap at the sandy shore. As you turn from the water to the cliffs behind, you notice the entrance to a large cave in the face of the black rock. You decide to enter the cave, feeling completely safe and secure, for that is the nature of this cave.

Walking into the cave, you notice small sparks of light embedded in the ancient rock, giving off a soft glow and lighting your way. You move deeper into the cave, marveling at the air of peacefulness surrounding you. Up ahead you see a pink mist swirling around a large opening in the cave wall. With growing excitement, you walk to the pink mist....and then through it into a land of enchantment.

Greetings, traveler. You are now in the land called Framework 2, the magical place where all begins, where thoughts and feelings, beliefs and desires are *instantly* made manifest. Sense the magic of this wondrous place. Feel it sparkle all around you. Feel it tingle your fingertips. See its delight reflected on your face, with eyes open wide and lips smiling in wonder at this mystical land, this land where emerald trees shimmer with radiance, where the ground is covered in a soft pink mist and diamond bright stars glitter against a warm azure sky.

You walk down a winding path lined with flowers, watching your pleasant thoughts materialize into delightful scenes of nature—a white lily floating on the still pond here, a small animal wiggling its nose in greeting there. Around your neck appears a long necklace of silver cord on which are strung five brilliantly colored gems. And as you reach up and touch the first stone, a glowing white sphere emanating sparks of gold, you know you've been given the *power* of creation with this precious gift. As your fingers caress it, your whole body becomes illuminated by the knowledge that you have the *power* to create whatever it is you choose.

The next gem on the silver chord is the color of midnight blue shot through with sparks of violet. As you touch it lightly, you realize it reflects the *power* of the moment, the ability to consciously choose what you want to manifest and to start the process in this immediate moment. This *power* moves into your body, settles into your cells and becomes a part of you.

Your fingers move on to the next precious stone, a vivid red oval alive with the *power* of desire. And as you lightly caress this awesome gift, you know that desire is a necessary ingredient for consciously creating what you want. It is strong desire for the object or event of your choice that starts the manifestation process, and strong desire that brings it to fruition. Feel your body filling with the *power* to manifest strong desire, and the *power* to project it outward into Framework 2.

Next to the red oval of desire lies a gem the color of a powder-blue morning glory. As the sun awakens the morning glory, so your imagination awakens your creation, breathing life into it, adding substance and form. Imagination prepares your creation for delivery into physical reality. Feel the coolness of the blue stone of imagination, and let its *power* filter into your body, at first slowly, and then with a great magnifying force.

On your fingers move to the last gem on the silver chord, a deep green stone radiantly alive with the *power* of belief. Believe your creation can happen! Believe it with all your heart! Let the sureness of belief enter your soul, let the deep green of it flow over your body and be absorbed. For with the *power* of belief, your vision becomes a reality.

As you gather these five incredible gifts—the *power* of creation, the *power* of the moment, the *powers* of desire, imagination, and belief—in both hands and hold them closely to your chest, a brilliant white light emanates from your hands up to your face and settles upon your features like a fine veil of spun cloud. This is the veil of intuitive understanding. You now know how reality is created. You now *know* the truth of the universe.

With the confidence of attainment in your eyes, think of what you want to create. First see your wish as words, and see them form against the backdrop of your mind. Aware of the vivid red stone of desire around your neck, say these words again and again with desire, strong desire!

Now project the powder blue light of imagination out from you, and see it form your wish in Framework 2. This is your future! Feel happiness, feel exuberance and joy! Imbue your creation with great desire. Focus on it. Expect it. Assume it will happen!

Hold the intensity of emotion and project it into Framework 2. Give yourself at least two minutes to create your vision in this place of magic, and then bid it farewell. Back away from your creation mentally. Let it become a living thing separate from you, well tended by your inner self in Framework 2, awaiting the appropriate moment to enter physical reality. And just know, *know*, that it will happen. Your life is your own definition. What you put energy behind will be created. Feel the integrity of this in your mind, and then let it go...let it go. You've completed your work for today. Feel good about it, feel excited! Feel *powerful*.

Pioneers Becoming Wizards

That completes the suggestions, exercises and techniques to be found in this book. After all is said and done, after pages galore have been written about how to change, after numerous exercises have been discussed, it all boils down to one simple fact: Change your mind, change your life. It's true that to get to the point of change may take new knowledge and ideas that open perceptions long closed, but the bottom line is clear.

Some day our race will be wizards at conscious creation, but right now we're pioneers. We're only beginning to learn how to direct the power of our minds. But learn we will, because it's the next step in the evolution of our race, and the alternative is too dismal to contemplate.

So, change your mind, change your life...change the world.

9

When man realizes that he, himself, creates his personal and universal environment in concrete terms, then he can begin to create a private and universal environment much superior to the (present) one, that is a result of haphazard and unenlightened constructions. This is our main message to the world, and this is the next line in man's conceptual development...
—*Seth*, The "Unknown" Reality, Volume Two, *Epilogue*

Conscious Living

Every organism, including the amoeba, has the ability to create its life by translating ideas into idea constructions. That simple organism takes every idea it receives and, without thought or reflection, instantaneously constructs what it needs to survive on the physical plane. It doesn't know itself as a separate entity apart from its environment; it senses its environment and understands it is one with it.

Much more complicated organisms, such as animals, similarly know they are one with their surroundings, and yet they sense their individuality, also. They receive many more ideas than the simpler organisms and handle them differently. For instance, in order to create their existence, they reflect briefly on ideas to determine which to manifest—and the result is the first tracings of choice and decision found in consciousness. The result is also the first suggestion of time awareness found in consciousness, for to reflect means to pause.

Then, up the scale of complicated organisms stands mankind—and I use the term generically. Man is so receptive to ideas that he is barraged by them constantly. As his consciousness expanded and more and more ideas followed, he realized he could not possibly construct all of them into physical reality. What was needed was a screen through which to make decisions and choices, and so conscious purpose resulted. Then memory was conceptualized and developed so that idea constructions could be thought of as separate from each other, providing man with a basis for comparison and selection.

This compartmentalizing of idea constructions blossomed into a belief in linear time because memory seemed to suggest past experience—and so time continuity became an assumption by developing man. This naturally led to the birth of ego-consciousness as man started to see his identity as separate from his idea constructions, since he remained in the moment and they came and went. Ego-consciousness freed him to make selections for materialization into his reality based on desire and focus.

A problem occurred as man began to divorce himself more and more from the world of his constructions, eventually seeing them as something apart from his creation. Even though this was an artificial division, it nonetheless started to alienate him from nature, and a search for a mythic figurehead which could be assigned the role of Creator ensued. Gods and Goddesses were placed throughout time by man to symbolize the inner reflection of his origins.

While at times these symbols helped assuage the loneliness that grew from not remembering his oneness with all things, man still knew in his soul that something was amiss. Some of the race, more alienated than others perhaps, turned from theology and mythology to mechanistic answers—and so aligned themselves with modern science which verified their belief in complete removal from their source and nature.

The good news is that man can never divorce himself from himself; the bad news is that he can create the illusion of separation through his beliefs. What results, however, is a globe full of haphazard constructions created by the likes of hatred, bigotry, depression, anger, cynicism and fear; and fueled by beliefs in luck, fate and circumstances beyond control.

Our race is at an extremely important point in its psychic evolution. It has taken its belief in separation from its source just about as far as it can without creating its own destruction, at least in this shared mass reality we find ourselves in today. We will continue to do untold damage to civilization and nature until we stop seeing our idea constructions as separate from ourselves— and ourselves as separate from the source of our world.

The solution to changing the world now experienced by man is for man to re-create it in a new mold. That re-creation, without question, demands that we once again acknowledge the inner reality from which the outer reality springs. Until we know, intellectually and intuitively, that creation happens first in the inner world and then appears in the outer world, and that we, in conjunction with our inner selves, are the powerhouses behind that creation, no sustained changes will occur on a global scale. They can't. It's that simple.

Global events are formed just as individual ones are, but they are formed by the mass beliefs of all souls alive in physical reality. The great dramas that have crossed the centuries, such as the Holocaust, the Renaissance, the birth of America and apartheid in South Africa, could not have occurred unless a lot of individual thoughts, attitudes and beliefs had coalesced into mass events.

To alter beliefs on a mass level takes many people imbued with the same understandings. It takes the magnification of one individual's reality combined with many others to launch mass reactions. Periods of great art and technology were started in this way, as were new cultural periods and the births of religions. So were acts of genocide, the sweep of deadly epidemics and war's mass murders. We get what we believe is possible and probable, individually and en masse.

The answer to world change becomes private change. As each of us sheds our beliefs in vulnerability, victimization and the need for aggression, and replaces them with beliefs in complete security and inner strength, our world lights up with hope—because it's one less person feeding negativity into the world psychic gestalt of consciousness, and it's one more person feeding the same gestalt with love and peace.

As Seth reminds us, "The race suffers when any of its members die of starvation or disease, even as a whole plant suffers if a group of its leaves are "unhappy." In the same way all members of the species are benefited by the happiness, health, and fulfillment of any of those individuals who compose it...One part of the species cannot grow or develop at the expense of the other portions for very long."[1]

The Doorway to Knowledge

Each evolutionary change is preceded and caused by a new idea. Perhaps the most important idea we need to accept in order to launch a massive shift in world conditions is that *we are multidimensional entities active in both time and nontime simultaneously.* When we remember that we straddle realities, that we use the outer to learn the manipulation of energy into concrete objects and events that are decided upon and formed first in the inner, then we stop identifying so completely with the ego, and new flexibility is brought to our minds.

Individually we can only go so far through the more common intellectual and creative channels and then must open to other stimuli. When we cease to rely upon answers that have been given to us by others, we automatically open new channels of information always available, if we but know it. The inner senses are methods of perception that lead to those inner pathways of knowledge. They put us in immediate touch with our inner self, and from it comes great assistance and wisdom. If this conscious awareness of our inner self doesn't convince us of our multidimensionality, nothing will.

To experience great leaps in intuitive understanding takes the ability to look inward, to concentrate to the point of softening the edges of the physically-oriented self, and an intense desire to learn. Combined with the confidence that knowledge can be directly received from the inner self, conditions are brought about for the passage of information through the inner senses. This doorway to knowledge is always open, but we must desire it. Those who are certain of the answers won't ask, and so the door remains closed to them. Those who refuse to change their beliefs don't even notice a door.

We must use the conscious mind with clarity and come to rely on its assessment of our exterior world. This means the conscious mind, buoyed by undistorted knowledge, must be used as completely as possible, with its snapshot of the outer world uncolored by raging emotions. The point of being consciousness in a physical reality is to see our idea constructions made manifest, and decide what does and does not work for us, or what we do or do not wish to experience. In other words, the point of being physical is to come to a *conscious* understanding of how our thoughts literally take on form. Seth says we must learn this lesson well, because we need to fully understand the implications of creation before we can move on to other lessons in other places.

The conscious mind is a most valuable tool and should not be treated as the unrepentant stepchild of our uplifted spiritual natures. There is no division between intuitional and intellectual knowledge. It is only our misinterpretation of outer reality that has caused us to believe self-consciousness, or the ego, is a thing to be dominated and controlled.

It is true that when the ego becomes rigid it very effectively locks us into thought systems that take us nowhere we want to go. It's not that the ego needs taming. All it needs is new understandings through which to filter exterior experiences. The ego must become consciously aware of far more of the reality in which it finds itself. To do so, it eventually must shed the ideas of one self, one body, one world, one god, one timeline. It must become aware of probable pasts and probable futures, and learn to consciously select its direction.

Conscious Living

If time is simultaneous and we're surrounded by every probability that can ever occur, that suggests there are also unlimited worlds we can inhabit through our unlimited selection of probabilities. There's one where no hunger exists, because we understand our intense power to create whatever we need; and there's one where the race dies from the face of the earth because there is no food to be had. There's a world where peace reigns and the word *war* has no meaning; and there is one where war reigns and the word *peace* is vaguely remembered from antiquity.

Thank goodness the means of reaching our destination of choice, the civilization we wish to experience, is part of our racial make-up. We have inner codes imbedded in our psyches that are patterns or models depicting man's greatest potentials and possible achievements. The inner codes are what draw us into the future, because as consciousness we seek to actualize them, growing into ourselves in the process. We unfold as we strive to become living embodiments of our potential inherent in the inner codes. We seek the blueprint for our growth as flowers seek sun. Unless we become rigid in our thinking and inflexible in our belief systems, we can be guided and prodded into a new world.

The choice is ours, the prize is ours. Becoming conscious creators, and all it implies, is the path.

Notes

Introduction

1. A complete listing of books by Jane Roberts and Seth is found in "Suggested Reading."

Chapter 1: The 180-Degree Turn

1. A gestalt is defined by *Webster's New Collegiate Dictionary* as "...a structure, configuration, or pattern of physical, biological, or psychological phenomena so integrated as to constitute a functional unit with properties not derivable from its parts in summation."

2. Jane Roberts, *Seth, Dreams and Projection of Consciousness* (Walpole, N.H.: Stillpoint Publishing, 1986), Chapter 1, p. 49-51.

3. Jane Roberts, *The Seth Material* (New York: Prentice Hall Press, 1970), Chapter 10, p. 115.

4. Jane Roberts, *How to Develop Your ESP Power* (Hollywood, Florida: Lifetime Books, Inc., 1993), Chapter 4, p. 67.

Chapter 3: On a Moment's Notice

1. Jane Roberts, *The Seth Material* (New York: Prentice Hall Press, 1970), Chapter 10, p. 114.

2. Jane Roberts, *The Nature of Personal Reality* (San Rafael, Calif.: Amber-Allen/New World Library, 1994), Session 656.

3. Jane Roberts, *The Nature of Personal Reality* (San Rafael, Calif.: Amber-Allen/New World Library, 1994), Session 656.

4. Jane Roberts, *How to Develop Your ESP Power* (Hollywood, Florida: Lifetime Books, Inc., 1993), Chapter 4, p. 67.

Chapter 5: Power Hitters of the Universe

1. Jane Roberts, *Adventures in Consciousness: An Introduction to Aspect Psychology* (New York: Bantam Books, 1975), Chapter 18.

2. Jane Roberts, *The Nature of Personal Reality* (San Rafael, Calif.: Amber-Allen/New World Library, 1994), Session 645.

3. Jane Roberts, *The Nature of Personal Reality* (San Rafael, Calif.: Amber-Allen/New World Library, 1994), Session 623.

4. "Hollywood-At-Home," *Architectural Digest*, April, 1994.

5. Jane Roberts, *The Nature of Personal Reality* (San Rafael, Calif.: Amber-Allen/New World Library, 1994), Session 660.

6. "Linus Pauling, crusader for peace and healing powers of vitamin C," *USA Today*, 1994.

7. Jane Roberts, *The Nature of Personal Reality* (San Rafael, Calif.: Amber-Allen/New World Library, 1994), Session 654.

8. "Boomers' cancer risk tops grandparents," *USA Today*, 9 February, 1994.

9. "Healing power of placebo underestimated," *USA Today*, 25 May, 1994.

10. Jane Roberts, *The Nature of Personal Reality* (San Rafael, Calif.: Amber-Allen/New World Library, 1994), Session 623.

11. "Poll: More fear being murdered," *USA Today*, 26 November, 1993.

12. Sue Watkins, *Conversations with Seth, Volume 2* (New York: Prentice Hall Press, 1981), Chapter 19, p. 515.

Chapter 6: Minding the Magic of Life

1. Jane Roberts, *The God of Jane: A Psychic Manifesto* (Engle-

wood Cliffs, N.J.: Prentice-Hall, Inc., 1981), Chapter 2, p. 13.

2. Jane Roberts, *Seth Speaks: The Eternal Validity of the Soul* (San Rafael, Calif.: Amber-Allen/New World Library, 1994), Session 530.

3. Jane Roberts, *The Nature of Personal Reality* (San Rafael, Calif.: Amber-Allen/New World Library, 1994), Session 625.

4. Jane Roberts, *The Nature of Personal Reality* (San Rafael, Calif.: Amber-Allen/New World Library, 1994), Session 675.

5. Jane Roberts, *The Nature of Personal Reality* (San Rafael, Calif.: Amber-Allen/New World Library, 1994), Session 627.

Chapter 7: Consciously Creating Change

1. Jane Roberts, *The Nature of the Psyche: Its Human Expression* (San Rafael, Calif.: Amber-Allen Publishing, 1996), Session 764.

2. Jane Roberts, *The Nature of Personal Reality* (San Rafael, Calif.: Amber-Allen/New World Library, 1994), Session 660.

3. Jane Roberts, *The Nature of Personal Reality* (San Rafael, Calif.: Amber-Allen/New World Library, 1994), Session 658.

Chapter 8: Time Sculpting

1. Jane Roberts, *The Nature of Personal Reality* (San Rafael, Calif.: Amber-Allen/New World Library, 1994), Session 654.

2. Jane Roberts, *The Nature of Personal Reality* (San Rafael, Calif.: Amber-Allen/New World Library, 1994), Session 657.

3. Jane Roberts, *The Individual and the Nature of Mass Events* (San Rafael, Calif.: Amber-Allen Publishing, 1995), Session 806.

4. Jane Roberts, *The Nature of Personal Reality* (San Rafael, Calif.: Amber-Allen/New World Library, 1994), Session 654.

5. Jane Roberts, *The Nature of Personal Reality* (San Rafael, Calif.: Amber-Allen/New World Library, 1994), Session 675.

Chapter 9: Conscious Living

1. Jane Roberts, *The "Unknown" Reality, Volume One* (Englewood Cliffs, N.J.: Prentice-Hall, Inc., 1977), Session 697.

Suggested Reading

Books by Jane Roberts, Dictated by Seth

Roberts, Jane. *Seth Speaks: The Eternal Validity of the Soul*. Notes by Robert F. Butts. San Rafael, Calif.: Amber-Allen/New World Library, 1994.

___. *The Nature of Personal Reality: A Seth Book*. Notes by Robert F. Butts. San Rafael, Calif.: Amber-Allen/New World Library, 1994.

___. *The "Unknown" Reality: A Seth Book, Volume One*. Notes and Introduction by Robert F. Butts. San Rafael, Calif.: Amber-Allen Publishing, 1996.

___. *The "Unknown" Reality: A Seth Book, Volume Two*. Notes and Introduction by Robert F. Butts. San Rafael, Calif.: Amber-Allen Publishing, 1996.

___. *The Nature of the Psyche: Its Human Expression*. San Rafael, Calif.: Amber-Allen Publishing, 1996.

___. *The Individual and the Nature of Mass Events*. Notes by Robert F. Butts. San Rafael, Calif.: Amber-Allen Publishing, 1995.

___. *Dreams, "Evolution," and Value Fulfillment, Volume One*. Introductory Essays and Notes by Robert F. Butts. San Rafael, Calif.: Amber-Allen Publishing, 1997.

___. *Dreams, "Evolution," and Value Fulfillment, Volume Two*. Introductory Essays and Notes by Robert F. Butts. San Rafael, Calif.: Amber-Allen Publishing, 1997.

___. *The Magical Approach*: *Seth Speaks About the Art of Creative Living*. Notes by Robert F. Butts. San Rafael, Calif.: Amber-Allen/New World Library, 1995.

Books by Jane Roberts, Related to Her Work With Seth

Roberts, Jane. *How to Develop Your ESP Power*. Hollywood, Florida: Lifetime Books, Inc., 1993.

___. *The Seth Material*. New York: Prentice Hall Press, 1970.

___. *Adventures in Consciousness: An Introduction to Aspect Psychology*. Eugene, Ore.: SethNet Publishing, 1997.

___. *Dialogues of the Soul and Mortal Self in Time*. Englewood Cliffs, N.J.: Prentice-Hall, Inc., 1975.

___. *Psychic Politics: An Aspect Psychology Book*. Englewood Cliffs, N.J.: Prentice-Hall, Inc., 1976. (To be republished by SethNet Publishing, Eugene, Ore., in 1997.)

___. *The World View of Paul Cezanne*. Englewood Cliffs, N.J.: Prentice-Hall, Inc., 1977.

___. *The Afterdeath Journal of an American Philosopher: The World View of William James*. New York: Prentice Hall Press, 1978.

___. *Emir's Education in the Proper Use of Magical Powers*. Walpole, N.H.: Stillpoint Publishing, 1984.

___. *The God of Jane: A Psychic Manifesto*. Englewood Cliffs, N.J.: Prentice-Hall, Inc., 1981. (To be republished by SethNet Publishing, Eugene, Ore., in 1998.)

___. *If We Live Again: Or, Public Magic and Private Love*. New York: Prentice Hall Press, 1982.

___. *Seth, Dreams and Projections of Consciousness*. Walpole, N.H.: Stillpoint Publishing, 1986.

___. *The Oversoul Seven Trilogy: The Education of Oversoul Seven; The Further Education of Oversoul Seven; Oversoul Seven and the Museum of Time*. San Rafael, Calif.: Amber-Allen Publishing, 1995.

Additional Authors

Ashley, Nancy. *Create Your Own Reality: A Seth Workbook*. New York: Prentice Hall Press, 1987. (To be republished by SethNet Publishing, Eugene, Ore., in 1997.)

___. *Create Your Own Happiness: A Seth Workbook*. New York: Prentice Hall Press, 1988. (To be republished by SethNet Publishing, Eugene, Ore., in 1998.)

___. *Create Your Own Dreams: A Seth Workbook*. New York: Prentice Hall Press, 1990. (To be republished by SethNet Publishing, Eugene, Ore., in 1998.)

Friedman, Norman. *Bridging Science and Spirit: Common Elements in David Bohm's Physics, The Perennial Philosophy and Seth.* Eugene, Ore.: The Woodbridge Group, 1997.

___. *The Hidden Domain.* Eugene, Ore.: The Woodbridge Group, 1997.

Hay, Louise. *You Can Heal Your Body.* Carlsbad, Calif.: Hay House, Inc., 1982.

___. *You Can Heal Your Life*. Carlsbad, Calif.: Hay House, Inc., 1984.

Mawe, Sheelagh. *Dandelion: The Triumphant Life of a Misfit.* Orlando, Florida: Totally Unique Thoughts, 1987.

McDonald, John. *The Message of a Master*. San Rafael, Calif.: New World Library, 1993.

Perl, Sheri. *Healing From the Inside Out*. New York: NAL Penguin, Inc., 1988. (To be republished by SethNet Publishing, Eugene, Ore., in 1997.)

Stack, Rick. *Out-of-Body Adventures: 30 Days to the Most Exciting Experience of Your Life*. Chicago: Contemporary Books, Inc., 1988.

___. *The Early Sessions, Book 1 of The Seth Material*. Introduction and Notes by Robert F. Butts. Compiled by Rick Stack. Manhasset, NY: New Awareness Network Inc., 1997.

___. *The Early Sessions, Book 2 of The Seth Material*. Introduction and Notes by Robert F. Butts. Compiled by Rick Stack. Manhasset,

NY: New Awareness Network Inc., 1997.

Stone, Christopher. *Re-Creating Your Self.* Carlsbad, Calif.: Hay House, Inc., 1990.

Sheldon, Mary, and Christopher Stone. *The Meditation Journal.* West Hollywood, Calif.: Dove Books, 1996.

Watkins, Susan M. *Conversations With Seth: The Story of Jane Roberts's ESP Class, Volume One.* New York: Prentice Hall Press, 1986. (To be republished by SethNet Publishing, Eugene, Ore., in 1997.)

___. *Conversations With Seth: The Story of Jane Roberts's ESP Class, Volume Two.* New York: Prentice Hall Press, 1986. (To be republished by SethNet Publishing, Eugene, Ore., in 1998.)

___. *Dreaming Myself, Dreaming a Town.* New York: Kendall Enterprises, Inc., 1989. (To be republished by SethNet Publishing, Eugene, Ore., in 1998.)

About the Author

Lynda Dahl is president and chair of the Board of Directors of Seth Network International, vice president of The Woodbridge Group, and author of three books. A former computer industry vice president, she now lectures extensively on consciousness and has appeared on numerous radio and television shows. Lynda's immediate family includes her partner Stan Ulkowski, children Matthew and Cathleen, and cats galore.

SETH NETWORK INTERNATIONAL

Seth Network International (SNI) is a network of Seth/Jane Roberts readers from over 30 countries who meet to explore the ideas and share the excitement of the Seth material. SNI, a nonprofit company established in late 1992, provides the meeting place, or forum, for the gathering. Its primary purpose is to offer Seth readers a platform for expression and discussion.

SNI publishes a quarterly magazine, *Reality Change: The Global Seth Journal;* holds conferences each year; and offers The Brass Ring Bookstore, a mail-order catalog filled with Seth/Jane Roberts books, art, audiotapes and videotapes, and products by other authors. In 1996 SethNet Publishing, a division of SNI, was formed to publish some of Jane Roberts's books and other books compatible with the concepts found in the Seth material.

You can find SNI on CompuServe (GO NEWAAGE), where an on-line conference is held weekly at 6:30 p.m. Pacific Standard Time, and where you can peruse a library of Seth-related articles and follow ongoing discussions on the message board. On SNI's World Wide Web home page you will find almost 100 screens of information on the latest happenings around the Seth material and Seth Network International (http://www.efn.org/~sethweb). For The Brass Ring Bookstore catalog or further information, please contact:

Seth Network International
PO Box 1620
Eugene, OR 97440 USA
Phone (541) 683-0803 Fax (541) 683-1084